Baking Bliss

Essential Recipes for Perfect Pastries and Breads

FELICIA TENNY

The presentation of the information is without contract or any type of guarantee assurance. The trademarks that are used are without any consent, and the publication of the trademark is without permission or backing by the trademark owner. All trademarks and brands within this book are for clarifying purposes only and are the owned by the owners themselves, not affiliated with this document.

Table of Contents

Chapter 1

Introduction

The Joy and Art of Baking

Baking is an age-old craft that has woven itself into the fabric of human culture and tradition. It encompasses more than just the methodical combining of ingredients; it is an art form that brings joy, satisfaction, and a sense of accomplishment. The process of baking can be therapeutic, a way to express creativity, and a means to connect with others. From the precise measurements to the aromatic rewards, baking transforms a collection of simple ingredients into something extraordinary.

The foundation of baking lies in the basic ingredients: flour, sugar, eggs, butter, and leavening agents. Each element plays a crucial role in the final product. Flour provides the structure, sugar adds sweetness and color, eggs offer richness and stability, butter imbues flavor and tenderness, and leavening agents like baking powder or yeast create the rise and texture. Understanding how these ingredients interact is the first step in mastering the art of baking.

Precision is paramount in baking. Unlike cooking, where a dash of this or a pinch of that can be adjusted to taste, baking requires exact measurements. A kitchen scale becomes an invaluable tool, ensuring consistency and accuracy. Even slight deviations in ingredient quantities can alter the texture, appearance, and taste of the final product. Therefore, following recipes meticulously, at least until one becomes more experienced, is crucial.

Temperature control is another critical aspect. Ingredients should often be at room temperature unless otherwise specified. Butter, for example, should be soft but not melted for most cookie recipes, as its texture affects the dough's consistency. Oven temperature is equally important. Preheating the oven ensures that the baked goods cook evenly from the start. An oven thermometer can help verify that your oven's internal temperature matches the dial setting, as many ovens can be off by several degrees.

The method of mixing ingredients can also significantly impact the outcome. Creaming butter and sugar, for instance, incorporates air into the batter, resulting in a lighter, fluffier texture. Over-mixing, however, can develop the gluten in flour too much, making cakes or muffins dense and tough. Folding in ingredients gently for delicate batters or kneading dough to develop gluten for bread are techniques that bakers must master through practice and patience.

Baking is not just a science but also an art. The creative aspect comes into play when selecting flavors, designing decorations, and experimenting with new recipes. Combining different spices, fruits, nuts, or extracts can create unique and delightful flavors. Decorating cakes, cookies, and pastries allows for personal expression and can turn a simple dessert into a work of art. Piping intricate designs with frosting, glazing with a shiny finish, or dusting with powdered sugar can elevate the visual appeal of baked goods.

One of the most joyous aspects of baking is sharing the results with others. Whether it's a birthday cake, holiday cookies, or a simple loaf of bread, baked goods have a way of bringing people together. The act of giving something homemade conveys care and thoughtfulness. Hosting a bake sale, participating in a cookie swap, or baking for a community event are ways to spread joy and foster connections through baking.

Baking can also be a deeply personal and therapeutic activity. The rhythmic motions of mixing, kneading, and rolling can be meditative, allowing one to focus and unwind. The satisfaction of seeing a dough rise, a cake bake to perfection, or the first bite of a warm cookie can be immensely rewarding. Baking can provide a sense of accomplishment and a tangible result of one's efforts.

For beginners, starting with simple recipes is advisable. Classic chocolate chip cookies, banana bread, or a basic sponge cake are excellent starting points. These recipes typically have straightforward steps and are forgiving of minor mistakes. As confidence and skills grow, more complex recipes can be attempted, such as laminated dough for croissants, intricate pastries, or multi-layered cakes.

Experimentation and learning from mistakes are part of the baking journey. Not every attempt will be successful, but each provides a learning opportunity. Understanding why a cake sank in the middle, why cookies spread too much, or why bread didn't rise can help improve future bakes. Resources such as cookbooks, online tutorials, and baking classes can offer valuable guidance and tips to refine techniques and troubleshoot issues.

In addition to traditional baking, exploring different cultural baking traditions can be enlightening and enriching. Each culture has its own unique baked goods and techniques, from French patisseries to Italian biscotti, from Japanese mochi to Middle Eastern baklava. Trying recipes from around the world can expand one's baking repertoire and introduce new flavors and methods.

Sustainability in baking is another important consideration. Choosing locally sourced and seasonal ingredients can reduce the environmental impact. Using whole grains, reducing sugar, and incorporating natural sweeteners can make baked goods healthier. Minimizing waste by using leftovers creatively, such as turning stale bread into breadcrumbs or croutons, is another way to practice sustainable baking.

Baking with dietary restrictions in mind is also becoming increasingly important. Gluten-free, dairy-free, vegan, and low-sugar baking are areas where innovation is thriving. Alternative flours like almond, coconut, and rice flour can replace wheat flour. Plant-based substitutes for butter and eggs, such as coconut oil and flaxseed, allow for inclusive baking that caters to various dietary needs.

The tools and equipment used in baking can also enhance the experience. While a basic set of mixing bowls, measuring cups, and baking sheets is sufficient for beginners, investing in quality tools can make a significant difference. A stand mixer can simplify the process of mixing doughs and batters. Silicone baking mats provide a reusable, non-stick surface. Specialty pans and molds can create unique shapes and designs.

Baking is a lifelong learning process, with always new techniques to master and recipes to discover. Joining a baking community, whether online or in person, can provide support, inspiration, and a platform to share successes and challenges. Attending workshops, entering baking competitions, or simply exchanging recipes with friends can keep the passion for baking alive.

Ultimately, baking is about more than just creating delicious treats. It is a celebration of creativity, precision, and the joy of sharing. It bridges generations, cultures, and communities, bringing people together over the simple pleasure of something homemade. The art of baking, with its blend of science and creativity, offers endless opportunities for exploration and enjoyment. Whether you are baking for yourself, your family, or your friends, the joy and art of baking is a journey worth embarking on. Furthermore, the impact of baking extends beyond the kitchen and into the broader community. Participating in or organizing bake sales for charitable causes is a wonderful way to contribute to society. Schools, churches, and community centers often host such events, where the proceeds support various initiatives. Baking for these events not only raises funds but also fosters a spirit of generosity and involvement.

Essential Tools and Ingredients

Creating culinary masterpieces requires a solid foundation of essential tools and ingredients. Just as an artist needs the right brushes and paints, a cook needs the right utensils and ingredients to craft delicious dishes. This chapter explores the indispensable items every kitchen should have, ensuring that both novice and experienced cooks can prepare meals with ease and confidence.

A well-equipped kitchen begins with quality knives. A chef's knife, paring knife, and serrated knife form the holy trinity of cutting tools. The chef's knife, with its broad and sharp blade, is versatile for chopping vegetables, slicing meat, and mincing herbs. The paring knife excels at more delicate tasks such as peeling and trimming. The serrated knife effortlessly slices through bread and tomatoes without crushing them. Keeping these knives sharp is crucial; a dull knife is not only inefficient but more dangerous, as it requires more force and can slip unpredictably. A good honing steel and a whetstone or a professional sharpener will keep your blades in top condition.

Cutting boards are the unsung heroes of the kitchen. Wooden boards are gentle on knives and ideal for most tasks, while plastic boards are excellent for handling raw meat and fish due to their ease of sanitization. Having multiple cutting boards helps prevent cross-contamination, ensuring food safety. Additionally, a large cutting board provides ample space to work efficiently, while a smaller one can be handy for quick tasks.

Mixing bowls are another fundamental tool. Stainless steel bowls are lightweight, durable, and non-reactive, making them suitable for a wide range of uses, from mixing batters to tossing salads. Glass bowls, while heavier, allow you to see your ingredients and their progress. A set of nesting bowls, which fit inside each other for easy storage, offers versatility and convenience.

Measuring cups and spoons are essential for both baking and cooking. Accurate measurements are crucial, especially in baking, where precision can make or break a recipe. Dry measuring cups are designed for ingredients like flour and sugar, while liquid measuring cups, often with a spout, are used for water, oil, and other liquids. Measuring spoons cover smaller quantities and are indispensable for spices and baking powder. Investing in a digital kitchen scale can further enhance accuracy, particularly for bulk ingredients or recipes that use metric measurements.

Cookware is the backbone of your kitchen arsenal. A variety of pots and pans allows you to tackle any recipe. A good set includes a non-stick skillet for delicate tasks like cooking eggs, a stainless steel skillet for searing meat, and a cast iron skillet for high-heat cooking and oven use. Saucepans in various sizes, a stockpot for soups and stews, and a Dutch oven for braising and baking round out the essentials. Each type of cookware offers distinct advantages: non-stick surfaces make for easy cleanup, stainless steel conducts heat evenly, and cast iron retains heat exceptionally well.

Baking sheets and roasting pans are crucial for oven tasks. Rimmed baking sheets are versatile, used for everything from cookies to roasting vegetables. A heavy-duty roasting pan with a rack is perfect for meats and poultry, allowing for even cooking and easy drippings collection for gravy.

Small appliances can significantly enhance your kitchen's functionality. A reliable blender can puree soups, make smoothies, and even crush ice. An immersion blender offers convenience for blending directly in pots and bowls. A food processor is invaluable for chopping, slicing, and grating large quantities of ingredients quickly. Stand mixers are a baker's best friend, effortlessly kneading dough and whipping cream. Additionally, a slow cooker or Instant Pot can simplify meal preparation, allowing for hands-off cooking of complex dishes.

Beyond tools, a well-stocked pantry forms the cornerstone of any kitchen. Staple ingredients ensure you are always ready to create a meal, even on short notice. Flour, sugar, and baking powder are essential for baking, while a variety of oils (such as olive, vegetable, and sesame) and vinegars (like balsamic, apple cider, and white wine) provide the foundation for dressings and marinades. Spices and herbs add flavor and depth to dishes; a basic collection might include salt, pepper, garlic powder, paprika, cumin, and dried oregano. Fresh herbs like basil, cilantro, and parsley can elevate a dish but should be used promptly for maximum flavor.

Canned goods offer convenience and a long shelf life. Tomatoes in various forms (diced, crushed, paste) are versatile for sauces and soups. Beans, such as black beans, chickpeas, and lentils, are protein-rich and can be used in salads, stews, and dips. Broths and stocks, whether homemade or store-bought, provide a flavorful base for soups and risottos.

Grains and pasta are pantry staples that add bulk and substance to meals. Rice, quinoa, couscous, and a variety of pasta shapes allow for diverse culinary creations. Keeping a selection of these on hand ensures you can quickly prepare a satisfying base for any dish.

Refrigerated essentials include dairy products like milk, butter, and cheese, which are fundamental in many recipes. Eggs are incredibly versatile, used in baking, as a binding agent, or as a main ingredient. Fresh vegetables and fruits should be replenished regularly to ensure vibrant, nutritious meals. Carrots, onions, and celery, known as the holy trinity of mirepoix, are the foundation for countless recipes. Leafy greens, bell peppers, and tomatoes add color and nutrients.

Frozen foods can be lifesavers, providing quick meal options and preserving seasonal produce. Frozen vegetables retain their nutritional value and can be added directly to dishes. Fruits like berries can be used in smoothies or desserts. Having a few frozen proteins, such as chicken breasts or shrimp, ensures you have the main component of a meal ready to go.

Organization is key to maintaining a functional kitchen. Clear storage containers for dry goods, labeled and easily accessible, prevent pantry chaos and make it easier to see when supplies are running low. A spice rack or drawer organizer keeps spices in order and within reach. Keeping your refrigerator and freezer tidy, with items grouped by category, helps prevent food waste and streamline meal prep.

Lastly, don't overlook the importance of cleaning tools. A clean kitchen is a productive kitchen. Sponges, dishcloths, and scrub brushes are everyday essentials, while a sturdy dish rack and drying mat make cleanup efficient. All-purpose cleaners and sanitizing wipes keep surfaces safe and hygienic. Regular maintenance of your tools and appliances, such as descaling the coffee maker or wiping down the oven, ensures they remain in good working order.

By equipping your kitchen with these essential tools and ingredients, you set yourself up for success in all your culinary endeavors. Whether you are preparing a simple weeknight dinner or an elaborate feast, having the right equipment and supplies at your fingertips makes the process smoother and more enjoyable. The investment in quality tools and a well-stocked pantry pays off in the ease and pleasure of cooking, allowing you to focus on creativity and the joy of sharing delicious meals with others. Cooking is not just about following recipes; it's about improvisation and adapting to what you have on hand. With the right tools and ingredients, you can experiment and create dishes tailored to your tastes and dietary needs. A well-equipped kitchen empowers you to be resourceful, reducing the need for last-minute grocery runs and enabling you to make the most of seasonal produce and pantry staples.

Tips for Success in Baking

Baking is both an art and a science, requiring precision, patience, and a touch of creativity. While cooking allows for a degree of improvisation, baking demands strict adherence to recipes and techniques. Success in baking hinges on understanding the fundamental principles and executing them with care. Here are some indispensable tips to help you achieve consistent and delicious results in your baking endeavors.

One of the most critical aspects of baking is accurate measurement. Unlike cooking, where you can often eyeball ingredients, baking requires exact amounts to ensure the correct chemical reactions occur. Invest in a good set of measuring cups and spoons for dry ingredients and a liquid measuring cup for wet ingredients. Better yet, use a digital kitchen scale to weigh your ingredients. This method provides the highest level of accuracy, especially for ingredients like flour, which can vary significantly in volume depending on how it's scooped.

Temperature plays a crucial role in baking. Ingredients like butter and eggs often need to be at room temperature to blend properly and create the desired texture. Planning ahead and taking these ingredients out of the refrigerator well before you start can make a significant difference. On the flip side, certain pastries and doughs require cold ingredients and a cool working environment to achieve flaky layers. Understanding the temperature requirements of your recipe and adhering to them is key.

Proper mixing techniques are essential for developing the right structure in baked goods. Overmixing can lead to tough, dense results, especially in recipes that rely on the delicate balance of gluten formation, such as cakes and muffins. When combining dry and wet ingredients, mix just until incorporated. Folding, rather than stirring vigorously, helps maintain the airiness in batters. For doughs, kneading develops gluten, but it's important to know when to stop. For example, bread dough benefits from extensive kneading, while pie crusts and biscuits require minimal handling to stay tender.

Leavening agents like baking powder, baking soda, and yeast are the powerhouses behind the rise in your baked goods. Baking powder and baking soda need to be measured accurately and used in the right proportions. Baking soda requires an acidic component to activate, while baking powder contains both an acid and a base and only needs moisture. Yeast, a living organism, needs the right environment to thrive. Warm water and a bit of sugar help activate it, but water that's too hot can kill the yeast, preventing the dough from rising.

Preheating the oven is a step that should never be skipped. Many baked goods begin cooking the moment they enter the oven, and an inaccurate starting temperature can throw off the entire process. Using an oven thermometer can help ensure your oven is at the correct temperature, as many built-in oven gauges can be off by a few degrees. Understanding your oven's quirks, such as hot spots, can also help you adjust baking times and positions to achieve even results.

The quality of ingredients significantly impacts the final product. Fresh, high-quality ingredients lead to better flavors and textures. For instance, using real vanilla extract rather than imitation can make a noticeable difference in taste. The same goes for using fresh spices, high-quality chocolate, and fresh fruits. Whenever possible, opt for organic and unprocessed ingredients.

Knowing when your baked goods are done is a skill that develops over time. Visual cues, such as a golden-brown color, and tactile indicators, like a cake springing back when lightly touched, are helpful. Toothpick tests, where a toothpick inserted into the center of the baked good comes out clean or with a few crumbs, are also reliable. For breads, a hollow sound when tapped on the bottom indicates doneness. Investing in an instant-read thermometer can provide extra assurance, especially for items like bread and custards, where internal temperature is crucial.

Cooling is an often-overlooked step but is vital for the final texture and flavor. Many baked goods continue to cook and set while cooling. Leaving items like cakes and cookies on the baking sheet or in the pan for a few minutes before transferring them to a wire rack prevents them from breaking apart. For items like cheesecakes and custards, a gradual cooling process in the oven with the door slightly ajar can prevent cracks and ensure a smooth texture.

Storing baked goods properly maintains their freshness and quality. Most cakes and cookies can be kept at room temperature in an airtight container. Bread is best stored in a cool, dry place, and should be wrapped in a cloth or paper bag to maintain its crust while preventing it from drying out. Items with perishable ingredients, like cream-based fillings or frostings, should be refrigerated. Understanding the best storage methods for each type of baked good extends their shelf life and maintains their taste and texture.

Experimentation and practice are essential for mastering baking. Start with simple recipes and gradually tackle more complex ones as you build your skills. Don't be afraid to make mistakes; they are valuable learning experiences. Keep notes on what works and what doesn't, including any adjustments you make to recipes. Over time, you'll develop a deeper understanding of how different ingredients and techniques affect your results.

Baking is also a communal activity. Sharing your baked goods with family and friends not only spreads joy but also provides feedback that can help you improve. Joining a baking group or class can offer additional support and inspiration. Engaging with a community of fellow bakers fosters a sense of camaraderie and opens you up to new ideas and techniques.

Incorporating a bit of creativity into your baking can yield delightful surprises. Experiment with flavors, such as adding citrus zest to a basic cake recipe or infusing herbs into a simple syrup for glazing. Play with textures by combining crunchy and creamy elements. Decorating your baked goods with a personal touch, be it through intricate piping or a rustic finish, adds an element of artistry.

Ultimately, the key to success in baking lies in understanding the principles, practicing diligently, and embracing the joy of the process. Each step, from measuring ingredients to the final presentation, contributes to the magic of creating something delicious and beautiful. With patience and persistence, you can master the art of baking and consistently produce treats that delight the senses and warm the heart. Baking also offers a wonderful opportunity to explore cultural and historical recipes, connecting you to traditions and stories from around the world. Trying your hand at French pastries, Italian biscotti, or Japanese matcha desserts not only enhances your skills but also broadens your culinary horizons. This exploration can be both educational and deeply satisfying, as you replicate the flavors and techniques that have been cherished for generations.

Understanding Different Types of Dough and Batters

Understanding the various types of dough and batters is fundamental to baking. Each type brings unique characteristics, textures, and flavors to the table. Grasping the differences and knowing how to work with each can elevate your baking skills and broaden your repertoire.

Doughs are generally stiffer than batters and can be divided into several categories: yeast doughs, unleavened doughs, and chemically leavened doughs. Yeast doughs, such as those used for bread, pizza, and some pastries, depend on yeast for leavening. Yeast ferments the sugars in the dough, producing carbon dioxide and alcohol, which cause the dough to rise and develop flavor.

Working with yeast doughs requires understanding fermentation and proofing. Fermentation is the initial rise, where the yeast activates and the dough doubles in size. Proper kneading is crucial during this stage to develop gluten, the protein that provides structure and chewiness. After fermentation, the dough is shaped and allowed to proof, or rise again, before baking. Proofing ensures the final product is light and airy. Temperature and humidity significantly affect yeast activity, so it's important to create an environment where yeast can thrive.

Unleavened doughs, such as those used for flatbreads and crackers, do not rely on leavening agents like yeast or baking powder. These doughs are typically simpler and quicker to prepare. The texture is usually denser and crispier. Techniques like rolling and docking (pricking the dough with a fork) help control how the dough bakes, preventing unwanted puffing and ensuring an even texture.

Chemically leavened doughs use baking powder or baking soda to achieve rise. These include quick breads, biscuits, and scones. The leavening agents react with moisture and heat to produce carbon dioxide, which helps the dough rise quickly. Overmixing can cause the dough to become tough, as it leads to excessive gluten development. It's vital to mix just until the ingredients are combined.

Batters, on the other hand, are generally thinner than doughs and can be categorized into pour batters and drop batters. Pour batters, such as those used for pancakes, waffles, and cakes, have a higher liquid content and are easy to pour. Achieving the right consistency is key; too thick, and the batter won't spread properly, too thin, and it won't hold structure. Mixing techniques vary, but generally, you want to mix just enough to combine ingredients without over-developing gluten, which can result in tough textures.

Drop batters, used for muffins, some cookies, and certain types of cakes, are thicker and need to be spooned or dropped onto a baking sheet or into a pan. These batters often rely on a balance of wet and dry ingredients to achieve the right consistency. Overmixing can be an issue here as well, leading to dense or rubbery results. When making drop batters, it's helpful to fold the ingredients together gently, maintaining as much air as possible to ensure a light and tender final product.

Each type of dough and batter has its own set of rules for successful preparation. For example, pie dough and pastry dough require cold ingredients and minimal handling to ensure a flaky texture. The cold fat, whether it's butter, shortening, or lard, creates layers as it melts during baking. Overworking the dough can cause the fat to warm up and integrate too much with the flour, leading to a tough crust. Using tools like a pastry cutter or food processor helps incorporate the fat without overhandling.

Choux pastry, used for éclairs and cream puffs, is a unique dough that starts on the stovetop. Water, butter, flour, and eggs are combined and cooked to form a thick, smooth paste. The high moisture content in choux pastry creates steam during baking, causing the dough to puff up. It's crucial to bake choux pastry at the right temperature to ensure it puffs and dries out properly, avoiding a soggy interior.

Understanding the role of ingredients in each type of dough and batter is also essential. Flour provides structure through gluten formation, while fats add tenderness and flavor. Sugar not only sweetens but also aids in browning and tenderizing. Eggs contribute moisture, structure, and richness, while leavening agents create rise. Liquids bind ingredients together and activate leavening agents. Knowing how these ingredients interact helps in troubleshooting and adjusting recipes.

For instance, if a cake batter is too dense, it might need more liquid or a bit more leavening agent. If cookies spread too much, reducing the sugar or increasing the flour could help. Understanding these interactions allows for better control over the final product.

Temperature control is another critical aspect. Cold ingredients can slow down yeast activity in doughs, while warm ingredients can speed it up. For batters, room temperature ingredients often mix more uniformly, creating a better texture. Baking times and temperatures must be followed closely to achieve the desired results. An oven thermometer can be invaluable for ensuring your oven is at the correct temperature.

Techniques like folding, kneading, creaming, and beating all impact the final texture and structure of doughs and batters. Folding gently incorporates ingredients without deflating air bubbles, crucial for delicate batters like meringues and soufflés. Kneading develops gluten in yeast doughs, providing structure and elasticity. Creaming butter and sugar together incorporates air, giving cakes and cookies a light texture. Beating eggs or egg whites adds volume and can create a lighter texture in cakes and soufflés.

While mastering different types of dough and batters might seem daunting at first, practice and observation are key. Pay attention to how each one behaves during mixing, rising, and baking. Take notes on what works and what doesn't, and don't be afraid to experiment. Baking is a science, but it's also an art that allows for creativity and personal expression.

In summary, understanding the different types of dough and batters, along with their specific techniques and ingredient roles, is crucial for successful baking. Each type brings unique characteristics that can be manipulated and perfected with practice. By mastering these fundamentals, you'll be well-equipped to tackle a wide range of recipes and create baked goods that are not only delicious but also showcase your skills and creativity. Another aspect of working with different types of dough and batters is understanding how to store and handle them properly. Freshness and proper handling can significantly impact the quality of your baked goods. For yeast doughs, refrigeration can slow down the fermentation process, which can be beneficial if you're making dough ahead of time. After the initial rise, punch down the dough to release excess gas, then cover it tightly and refrigerate. When you're ready to bake, allow the dough to come to room temperature and complete its final proofing.

Safety and Hygiene in the Kitchen

Cleanliness and safety in the kitchen are paramount to a successful and enjoyable cooking experience. Whether you're a seasoned chef or a beginner, adhering to fundamental safety and hygiene practices not only ensures delicious meals but also protects you and your loved ones from potential foodborne illnesses and accidents.

The foundation of kitchen safety begins with personal hygiene. Washing hands thoroughly with soap and water before, during, and after handling food cannot be overstated. This simple yet crucial step helps eliminate harmful bacteria and pathogens that can cause foodborne illnesses. Fingernails should be kept short and clean, and any cuts or wounds should be properly bandaged and covered with gloves to prevent contamination.

Equally important is maintaining a clean and organized kitchen environment. Countertops, cutting boards, and utensils should be cleaned and sanitized before and after use, especially when dealing with raw meat, poultry, or seafood. Cross-contamination is a major cause of foodborne illnesses, so it's essential to use separate cutting boards and knives for raw and cooked foods. Color-coded cutting boards can be a helpful tool to prevent cross-contamination—one color for raw meat, another for vegetables, and so on.

Proper food storage plays a significant role in kitchen hygiene. Perishable items should be stored in the refrigerator at the appropriate temperature, typically below 40°F (4°C). Raw meats should be placed on the bottom shelf to prevent their juices from dripping onto other foods. Leftovers should be stored in airtight containers and consumed within a few days to ensure freshness and safety. It's also a good practice to label containers with the date they were stored, so you can keep track of their shelf life.

Understanding and adhering to food safety guidelines during preparation is crucial. Thawing frozen foods in the refrigerator rather than on the countertop prevents the growth of harmful bacteria. Cooking foods to their recommended internal temperatures ensures that any harmful pathogens are killed. Using a food thermometer can help verify that foods have reached safe temperatures—165°F (74°C) for poultry, 145°F (63°C) for whole cuts of meat, and 160°F (71°C) for ground meats.

In addition to food safety, preventing accidents in the kitchen is paramount. Sharp knives should always be handled with care, and dull knives should be avoided as they require more force and are more likely to slip, causing injuries. When cutting, use a stable cutting board and curl your fingers inward to protect them. It's also wise to keep knives stored safely in a knife block or on a magnetic strip to prevent accidental cuts.

Kitchen fires are another common hazard. Never leave cooking food unattended, especially when using high heat or deep-frying. Keep flammable items such as kitchen towels and paper away from the stove. It's also essential to have a fire extinguisher accessible in the kitchen and to know how to use it. In case of a grease fire, never use water to extinguish it—covering the pan with a lid or using baking soda can help smother the flames.

Proper attire can also enhance safety in the kitchen. Avoid loose clothing and dangling jewelry that could catch on pot handles or catch fire. Wearing closed-toe shoes protects your feet from spills and dropped objects. Using oven mitts or potholders when handling hot pots and pans can prevent burns and scalds.

Ventilation is another aspect of kitchen safety that is often overlooked. Cooking can produce smoke and fumes that are not only unpleasant but also potentially harmful. Ensure your kitchen is well-ventilated by using an exhaust fan or opening windows to allow fresh air to circulate. This practice helps reduce the risk of respiratory irritation and keeps your kitchen environment pleasant.

Cleaning as you go is a habit that can greatly improve both safety and efficiency in the kitchen. By keeping your workspace tidy, you minimize the risk of accidents and make the cooking process more enjoyable. Wash dishes, wipe down surfaces, and put away ingredients and tools as you finish using them. This approach not only keeps your kitchen clean but also makes the post-cooking cleanup much more manageable.

Waste management is another critical component of kitchen hygiene. Dispose of food scraps and packaging promptly to prevent attracting pests. Use a covered trash can and empty it regularly to avoid unpleasant odors and potential health hazards. Recycling where possible helps reduce waste and supports environmental sustainability.

Understanding the importance of sanitation extends to kitchen tools and appliances. Dishwashers, refrigerators, ovens, and microwaves should be cleaned regularly to prevent the buildup of grime and bacteria. Pay special attention to spots that are often overlooked, such as refrigerator seals and microwave interiors. For appliances that come into contact with food, like blenders and mixers, ensure all parts are thoroughly cleaned and dried before storing.

Maintaining a pest-free kitchen is essential for hygiene. Store dry goods such as flour, sugar, and grains in airtight containers to prevent infestations. Regularly inspect your pantry for signs of pests and take immediate action if any are found. Keeping your kitchen clean and free of crumbs and spills is a crucial step in deterring pests.

Education and awareness are key components of kitchen safety and hygiene. Stay informed about the latest food safety guidelines and best practices, and don't hesitate to seek out additional resources or training if needed. Many local health departments offer food safety courses that can provide valuable knowledge and skills.

For those cooking for individuals with food allergies or sensitivities, extra precautions are necessary. Always read ingredient labels carefully and be mindful of cross-contact, where allergens can transfer from one food to another. Thoroughly clean all surfaces and utensils after preparing allergen-containing foods to prevent accidental exposure.

Encouraging a culture of safety and hygiene in the kitchen benefits everyone. If you're cooking with others, communicate clearly about tasks and responsibilities to avoid confusion and accidents. Teaching children basic kitchen safety and hygiene from a young age instills good habits that they can carry into adulthood.

Incorporating technology can also enhance kitchen safety. Timers and smart appliances can help prevent overcooking and reduce the risk of fires. Apps and digital thermometers provide accurate temperature readings to ensure foods are cooked safely. However, technology should complement, not replace, fundamental safety practices and vigilance.

Ultimately, the goal of maintaining safety and hygiene in the kitchen is to create a space where culinary creativity can flourish without compromising health or well-being. By following these guidelines and remaining mindful of potential hazards, you can enjoy the process of cooking and baking while ensuring that every meal is prepared in the safest and most hygienic manner possible. This commitment to kitchen safety not only enhances the quality of your food but also fosters a sense of confidence and joy in your culinary endeavors. Understanding how to properly handle and store kitchen chemicals and cleaning supplies is another critical aspect of maintaining a safe cooking environment. All cleaning agents, detergents, and chemicals should be stored in their original containers with clear labels and kept out of reach of children and pets. It's essential to follow manufacturer instructions for use and disposal to avoid hazardous reactions or contamination.

Chapter 2

Getting Started with Baking

Basic Baking Techniques

Baking is both an art and a science, requiring a blend of creativity, precision, and technique. For beginners, understanding the basic baking techniques is crucial to achieving consistent, delicious results. This chapter will guide you through essential methods and tips to build a strong foundation in baking.

The journey begins with understanding ingredients and their roles. Flour, the backbone of most baked goods, provides structure. Different types of flour, such as all-purpose, bread, and cake flour, have varying protein contents, affecting the texture of the final product. All-purpose flour, versatile and commonly used, strikes a balance between strength and tenderness. Bread flour, with higher protein content, results in chewier textures, ideal for yeast breads. Cake flour, with its low protein content, yields tender, delicate cakes.

Sugar, another fundamental ingredient, not only sweetens but also affects texture and color. Granulated sugar, browns cookies and cakes through caramelization, while brown sugar, with its higher moisture content, adds a chewy texture and rich flavor. Powdered sugar, often used in icings, dissolves easily, creating smooth textures.

Leavening agents, such as baking powder, baking soda, and yeast, are essential for rising. Baking soda, an alkaline compound, needs an acidic ingredient like buttermilk or vinegar to activate and produce carbon dioxide, creating rise. Baking powder contains both an acid and a base, activating with moisture and heat, making it suitable for recipes without additional acidic ingredients. Yeast, a living organism, ferments sugars, producing carbon dioxide and alcohol, which helps dough rise and develop flavor.

Butter and other fats contribute to flavor, tenderness, and moisture. In recipes requiring creaming, such as cookies and cakes, butter should be at room temperature to trap air when beaten with sugar, leading to a light, airy texture. Cold butter, used in pie crusts and biscuits, creates flaky layers by melting and releasing steam during baking.

Eggs, versatile and multifunctional, provide structure, leavening, color, and flavor. They should be at room temperature for even mixing. When beaten, eggs incorporate air, aiding in leavening. Yolks, rich in fat, add moisture and tenderness, while whites, when whipped, create volume and stability in meringues and soufflés.

Milk and other liquids, like water, juice, or yogurt, hydrate dry ingredients, dissolve sugar and salt, and contribute to the batter's or dough's consistency. They also aid in browning and flavor development. Whole milk, with its fat content, adds richness, while lower-fat options affect texture and moisture.

Salt, though used in small quantities, is vital for balancing sweetness and enhancing flavors. It also strengthens gluten in doughs, contributing to structure.

Accurate measuring is paramount in baking. Dry ingredients should be measured using appropriate cups and leveled off with a straight edge. Liquid ingredients require clear, graduated measuring cups, read at eye level. Weighing ingredients with a kitchen scale ensures precision, especially for flour, which can vary greatly when measured by volume.

Mixing techniques significantly impact the final product's texture. The creaming method, common in cookies and cakes, involves beating butter and sugar until light and fluffy, incorporating air for a tender crumb. The muffin method, used for quick breads and muffins, requires separately mixing wet and dry ingredients, then gently combining to avoid overmixing, which can result in tough textures.

Folding, a gentle technique, is essential when incorporating delicate ingredients like whipped cream or beaten egg whites. Using a rubber spatula, ingredients are carefully folded to retain air and volume. This method is crucial in recipes like soufflés and mousses.

Kneading, primarily used in yeast breads, develops gluten, giving the dough its structure and elasticity. It involves pressing and folding the dough repeatedly until smooth and elastic. Over-kneading can make dough tough, while under-kneading results in dense bread.

Resting and proofing times are critical, particularly in yeast baking. Allowing dough to rest after mixing lets gluten relax, making it easier to shape. Proofing, the final rise before baking, develops flavor and texture.

Dough should double in size, indicating proper fermentation.

Baking temperatures and times must be followed meticulously. Preheating the oven ensures even cooking from the start. Different baked goods require specific temperatures; for instance, cookies often bake at higher temperatures for shorter times, while bread bakes at lower temperatures for longer periods. Using an oven thermometer verifies accuracy, as oven temperatures can vary.

Testing for doneness varies by recipe. Cakes and quick breads should spring back when lightly pressed and a toothpick inserted in the center should come out clean. Cookies are done when edges are set and slightly golden. Bread should sound hollow when tapped on the bottom.

Cooling is an often overlooked but essential step. Cakes and breads should cool in the pan for a few minutes to set before transferring to a wire rack to cool completely. Cookies should rest on the baking sheet for a couple of minutes to firm up before moving to a rack.

Storing baked goods properly maintains freshness. Cookies and cakes can be stored in airtight containers at room temperature for a few days. Bread should be wrapped in plastic or stored in a bread box to prevent drying out. For longer storage, freezing is effective. Wrap items tightly and use within a few months for best quality.

Experimentation and practice are key to mastering baking. Every baker faces challenges, from dense cakes to flat cookies. Learning from these experiences, adjusting techniques, and understanding ingredient interactions lead to improvement and confidence.

Baking is a rewarding, creative process that brings joy to both the baker and those who enjoy the results. By understanding and applying these basic techniques, beginners can embark on a journey of discovery and delight in the kitchen. Whether baking for family, friends, or personal satisfaction, mastering these fundamentals ensures success and fosters a lifelong love of baking. Beyond the foundational techniques, developing a sense of intuition and confidence in the kitchen will elevate your baking skills. Trusting your instincts and learning to recognize subtle cues in dough texture, batter consistency, and even the scent of your baking can make a significant difference. These skills, honed over time and with practice, will transform you from a novice to a confident baker capable of tackling more complex recipes and creating your own culinary masterpieces.

Understanding Measurements and Conversions

Baking is a precise art where understanding measurements and conversions is crucial for achieving consistent and successful results. Without this foundational knowledge, even the most carefully followed recipes can go awry. This chapter will delve into the importance of accurate measurements, the differences between various measuring systems, and the methods for converting measurements to ensure every bake is a triumph.

In the world of baking, precision is key. Unlike cooking, where a dash of this or a pinch of that can be adjusted to taste, baking relies on exact measurements to maintain the delicate balance of ingredients. Understanding the differences between volume and weight measurements, as well as how to use measuring tools accurately, is essential for beginners and seasoned bakers alike.

Volume measurements are commonly used in recipes from the United States, with ingredients measured in cups, tablespoons, and teaspoons. While convenient, volume measurements can be less precise due to the varying densities of ingredients and the potential for user error. For example, a cup of flour can weigh differently depending on how it is scooped and leveled. To measure flour accurately, spoon it into the measuring cup and level it off with a straight edge without packing it down. This technique helps achieve a more consistent measurement, though it's still not as precise as weighing.

Weight measurements, on the other hand, provide greater accuracy. Ingredients are measured in grams or ounces, allowing for precise replication of recipes. A digital kitchen scale is an invaluable tool for any baker, enabling them to measure ingredients down to the gram. This precision is particularly important for ingredients like flour and sugar, where small variations can significantly impact the final product. When following a recipe that provides measurements by weight, simply place your mixing bowl on the scale, zero it out, and add the ingredients directly into the bowl, ensuring exact quantities.

Conversions between volume and weight measurements can be tricky but are often necessary, especially when using recipes from different regions or sources. For example, converting a recipe from the United States to the metric system requires understanding that one cup of all-purpose flour typically weighs around 120 grams, one cup of granulated sugar is approximately 200 grams, and so on. These conversions can vary slightly based on ingredient type and packing method, so having a reliable conversion chart or using a trusted online converter can be very helpful.

Besides flour and sugar, other common ingredients also require accurate measurement. Butter, for instance, is often measured in tablespoons or sticks in the United States, but in grams or ounces elsewhere. One stick of butter equals 113 grams or 4 ounces. For liquids, one cup is equivalent to 240 milliliters. Understanding these basic conversions allows for seamless recipe adaptation and ensures consistency in your baking.

Temperature is another crucial factor in baking, affecting how ingredients react and how the final product turns out. Oven temperatures are commonly given in Fahrenheit in the United States and Celsius elsewhere. To convert between the two, remember that 350°F is approximately 180°C. This conversion can be particularly important when following recipes from different countries. Additionally, ingredients like butter and eggs are often specified at room temperature, which generally means around 68-70°F (20-21°C). Ensuring ingredients are at the correct temperature can significantly impact the texture and structure of your baked goods.

When measuring liquids, using the right tools is essential. Liquid measuring cups, usually made of glass or clear plastic, are designed with spouts for easy pouring and measurement markings that are read at eye level. Measuring spoons are used for smaller quantities, and it's important to fill them to the brim and level them off for accuracy. For dry ingredients, nested measuring cups are used, and they should be filled to heaping and then leveled off with a straight edge.

Bakers also need to understand the importance of ingredient ratios and how they relate to the overall structure of the baked good. For example, the ratio of flour to liquid affects the dough or batter's consistency. Bread doughs typically have a higher flour-to-liquid ratio, resulting in a firmer texture, while cake batters have a higher liquid content for a softer, more tender crumb. Knowing these ratios helps bakers adjust recipes according to their needs or preferences.

Substitutions are sometimes necessary, whether due to dietary restrictions or ingredient availability. Understanding how to convert common substitutions can save a bake. For instance, if you need to replace one cup of buttermilk, you can mix one tablespoon of lemon juice or vinegar with enough milk to make up one cup and let it sit for a few minutes. Similarly, one cup of granulated sugar can be substituted with one cup of packed brown sugar, though this may slightly alter the flavor and moisture content of the final product.

Altitude can also affect baking, as higher elevations can cause baked goods to rise too quickly and then collapse. Adjusting recipes for high altitudes often involves reducing leavening agents, increasing liquid, and sometimes increasing the oven temperature slightly. Knowing how to make these adjustments ensures that your baked goods turn out well, regardless of where you are baking.

Maintaining accuracy in measurements and conversions is not just about following recipes to the letter but understanding the science behind baking. This understanding allows bakers to experiment with confidence, knowing how changes will affect the outcome. Whether converting measurements from one system to another, adjusting for altitude, or making ingredient substitutions, a solid grasp of measurements and conversions is an essential skill for any baker.

In summary, mastering measurements and conversions is fundamental to successful baking. Precision in measuring ingredients, understanding the differences between volume and weight, and knowing how to convert between systems are all critical components. By honing these skills, bakers can ensure their creations are consistently delicious and perfectly executed. This knowledge not only aids in following recipes accurately but also empowers bakers to adapt and experiment with confidence, leading to endless possibilities in the kitchen. Another critical aspect of understanding measurements and conversions in baking is the role of different types of ingredients and how they interact. For example, the difference between baking soda and baking powder can be confusing for beginners, but it's essential to grasp their distinct properties and how to measure them correctly. Baking soda is a single-ingredient leavening agent, while baking powder contains both an acid and a base, meaning it can leaven on its own. Using too much or too little of either can drastically affect the rise and texture of your baked goods.

The Role of Temperature in Baking

Temperature is one of the most critical factors in baking, influencing everything from the texture and flavor of your baked goods to the structure and rise. Whether you're a novice or an experienced baker, understanding how temperature affects your ingredients and the baking process can mean the difference between success and failure. This chapter will delve into the intricacies of temperature control, offering practical advice on managing and using temperature to your advantage.

At its core, baking is a series of chemical reactions, many of which are temperature-dependent. The most obvious example is the role of heat in transforming dough or batter into a finished product. When you place a cake or a loaf of bread into a preheated oven, several critical processes begin. Heat causes proteins and starches to set, fats to melt, and leavening agents to produce gas that gets trapped in the structure of the dough, causing it to rise. The Maillard reaction, responsible for the browning and complex flavors in baked goods, also kicks in at higher temperatures.

Preheating the oven is a step that should never be skipped. It ensures that the heat is evenly distributed and that your baked goods start cooking immediately upon entering the oven. Most recipes specify a preheating temperature, and adhering to this recommendation is crucial. An oven thermometer can be a valuable tool, as many home ovens are not perfectly calibrated and can be off by several degrees. Placing an oven thermometer inside will give you a more accurate reading, allowing you to adjust the dial as necessary.

Oven temperature is not the only temperature that matters; the temperature of your ingredients plays a significant role as well. Ingredients like butter, eggs, and milk should often be at room temperature unless specified otherwise. Room temperature ingredients blend more smoothly and evenly, leading to a better texture in your baked goods. For instance, room temperature butter creamed with sugar will hold air better, resulting in a lighter, fluffier batter.

Conversely, some recipes call for cold ingredients, particularly in pastry and pie doughs. Cold butter, when cut into flour, creates small, solid pieces that melt during baking, forming pockets of steam. These steam pockets produce the flaky layers characteristic of a good pie crust or puff pastry. Keeping ingredients cold in these cases prevents the butter from melting too soon and ensures a tender, flaky result.

Another critical aspect of temperature control is the initial mixing of ingredients. Over-mixing can cause the temperature of the dough or batter to rise, particularly in recipes requiring cold ingredients. For this reason, it's often advised to mix just until combined. Handling doughs lightly and minimally helps maintain the desired temperature and texture.

The temperature of your kitchen can also affect your baking. A warm kitchen can cause butter to soften too much, yeast to become overactive, or chocolate to melt prematurely. Conversely, a very cold kitchen can make it difficult for dough to rise or butter to cream properly. Being aware of your kitchen's environment and making adjustments as needed, such as chilling your mixing bowl or pre-warming your oven, can help mitigate these effects.

Fermentation is another process heavily influenced by temperature, particularly in bread baking. Yeast is a living organism that ferments and produces carbon dioxide gas, causing the dough to rise. The rate of fermentation is temperature-dependent: too cold, and the yeast will be sluggish; too warm, and it may become overactive, leading to over-proofing. The ideal temperature for yeast fermentation is around 75-78°F (24-26°C). Some advanced bakers use proofing boxes to maintain a consistent environment for their dough, but for home bakers, a warm (not hot) spot in the kitchen or an oven with the light on can suffice.

Baking times are often given as ranges rather than exact times, and this is partly due to variations in oven temperatures and the specific characteristics of your ingredients and environment. Keeping an eye on visual and tactile cues is essential. For example, cakes are done when they spring back to the touch and a toothpick inserted into the center comes out clean. Bread is finished baking when it sounds hollow when tapped on the bottom and registers an internal temperature of around 190-210°F (88-99°C), depending on the type.

Temperature control continues even after baking. Cooling your baked goods properly is crucial for the final texture and flavor. Cakes and cookies continue to set as they cool, and removing them from the baking sheet or pan too soon can cause them to fall apart. On the other hand, leaving them in the pan for too long can result in over-baking from residual heat. Using a wire cooling rack allows air to circulate around your baked goods, cooling them evenly and preventing sogginess.

Certain types of baked goods, like cheesecakes and custards, benefit from gradual cooling to prevent cracking. Turning off the oven and leaving the door ajar for a slow, gentle cooling process can help maintain their smooth, creamy texture. For chocolate-based desserts, cooling at room temperature rather than in the refrigerator helps preserve the glossy finish and prevents blooming, the white, streaky pattern that can form on the surface.

In the realm of advanced baking, temperature control becomes even more nuanced. Techniques like tempering chocolate require precise temperature management to achieve the right crystal structure, resulting in a shiny finish and a satisfying snap. Using a double boiler or a microwave with frequent stirring and temperature checks can help achieve perfect tempering.

Sous-vide baking is another advanced technique where batters and doughs are cooked in a water bath at a precise, controlled temperature. This method can produce incredibly moist and evenly baked results, though it requires specialized equipment and a deep understanding of temperature effects.

Understanding the role of temperature in baking is not just about following recipes meticulously but about developing an intuition for how temperature affects every ingredient and process. This knowledge allows bakers to troubleshoot issues, adapt recipes to their specific environments, and experiment with new techniques confidently.

Maintaining a baking journal can be a valuable practice, noting down temperature settings, ingredient temperatures, and environmental conditions for each bake. Over time, this record can help you identify patterns and make more informed adjustments, leading to consistently better results.

In conclusion, temperature is a multifaceted and vital aspect of baking that influences every stage of the process, from ingredient preparation to the final bake. By mastering temperature control, bakers can elevate their craft, ensuring that each creation is perfectly baked, with the desired texture, flavor, and appearance. This deep understanding of temperature's role in baking not only enhances the precision and reliability of your bakes but also opens up new avenues for culinary creativity and innovation. With temperature mastery, troubleshooting common baking issues becomes more intuitive. For instance, if your cake consistently domes in the middle, it could be a sign that your oven is too hot. The outer edges set too quickly while the center continues to rise, creating a dome. Lowering the oven temperature by 25°F (about 4°C) and extending the baking time can help achieve a more even rise.

Common Baking Mistakes and How to Avoid Them

Baking can be a rewarding and enjoyable experience, but it's also a science that requires precision and attention to detail. Even experienced bakers can make mistakes that can lead to disappointing results. Understanding common baking mistakes and how to avoid them is crucial for achieving consistent, delicious outcomes. This chapter will delve into some frequent errors that bakers make and provide practical strategies to sidestep them.

One of the most common mistakes in baking is not reading the recipe thoroughly before starting. Skimming through the instructions can lead to missing important steps or misinterpreting the order of operations. To avoid this, take the time to read the entire recipe from start to finish before beginning. This practice helps you understand the process, gather all necessary ingredients, and prepare the required equipment. It also allows you to identify any steps that might need extra attention or time, such as chilling dough or preheating the oven.

Measuring ingredients inaccurately is another frequent mistake. Baking is a precise science, and even small deviations in ingredient quantities can affect the final product. For dry ingredients like flour and sugar, use the spoon-and-level method: spoon the ingredient into the measuring cup and level it off with a flat edge. Avoid scooping directly from the container, as this can compact the ingredient and result in using too much. For liquid ingredients, use a clear measuring cup placed on a flat surface and check the measurement at eye level. Investing in a kitchen scale can further enhance accuracy, especially for ingredients like flour, which can vary significantly in weight depending on how it's packed.

Overmixing or undermixing batter is a common pitfall that can affect the texture of your baked goods. Overmixing can develop too much gluten in the flour, resulting in tough, dense products, while undermixing can leave lumps and pockets of unincorporated ingredients. To avoid these issues, mix just until the ingredients are combined. When incorporating dry ingredients into wet, fold gently with a spatula rather than using a vigorous stirring motion. For recipes that call for creaming butter and sugar, beat until the mixture is light and fluffy, which can take several minutes, but stop as soon as you reach the desired texture to prevent overworking the batter.

Temperature plays a critical role in baking, and not paying attention to it can lead to various problems. Using ingredients at the wrong temperature is a common mistake. Many recipes call for ingredients like butter, eggs, and milk to be at room temperature. Room temperature ingredients blend more easily and evenly, leading to a better texture. Plan ahead by taking these ingredients out of the refrigerator at least an hour before you start baking. Conversely, when cold ingredients are required, such as for making pastry dough, ensure they are kept chilled to achieve the desired flakiness.

Another temperature-related mistake is not preheating the oven properly. Placing your batter or dough in an oven that hasn't reached the specified temperature can affect the rise and texture of your baked goods. Always preheat your oven for at least 15-20 minutes before baking. Using an oven thermometer can help ensure your oven is at the correct temperature, as many ovens are not perfectly calibrated. Additionally, avoid opening the oven door frequently during baking, as this causes temperature fluctuations that can lead to uneven baking.

Ignoring the importance of sifting dry ingredients is another common error. Sifting aerates the flour, removes lumps, and ensures even distribution of leavening agents like baking powder and baking soda. This step is particularly important for delicate baked goods like cakes and pastries. If a recipe calls for sifted ingredients, don't skip this step. Sifting also helps to mix dry ingredients thoroughly, contributing to a uniform texture in the final product.

Using outdated leavening agents can result in flat, dense baked goods. Baking powder and baking soda lose their potency over time, especially if not stored properly. Check the expiration dates on these ingredients, and if they are past their prime, replace them. To test the freshness of baking powder, mix a small amount with hot water; it should fizz vigorously. For baking soda, mix with vinegar or lemon juice; it should bubble actively. Storing these ingredients in a cool, dry place in airtight containers can extend their shelf life.

Overcrowding the baking pan is a mistake that can lead to uneven baking. Cookies, for example, need space to spread, and cakes and bread need room to rise. If the pan is too crowded, the heat cannot circulate properly, resulting in some areas being undercooked while others might be overbaked. Follow the recipe's guidance on pan size and spacing. If you need to bake multiple batches, be patient and avoid the temptation to cram everything into one pan.

Incorrectly preparing pans can also cause issues. Failing to grease and flour the pan or using the wrong type of parchment paper can make it difficult to remove baked goods without breaking them. Always follow the recipe's instructions for preparing the pan. For cakes, greasing and flouring the pan or using parchment paper can prevent sticking. For cookies, using a silicone baking mat or parchment paper can ensure even baking and easy release.

Timing is critical in baking, and setting incorrect baking times is a common mistake. Trusting the recipe's time range without checking for doneness can lead to overbaking or underbaking. Set a timer but start checking for doneness a few minutes before the minimum recommended time. Use visual and tactile cues: cakes should spring back when lightly touched, cookies should be set around the edges but slightly soft in the center, and bread should sound hollow when tapped on the bottom. Using a toothpick or cake tester can help check if the item is baked through; it should come out clean or with a few moist crumbs, depending on the recipe.

Improper cooling of baked goods can affect their texture and flavor. Many items continue to cook from residual heat after being removed from the oven. Following cooling instructions is crucial; for example, cooling cakes in the pan for a specified time before turning them out onto a wire rack prevents them from breaking apart. Cookies should be allowed to set on the baking sheet for a few minutes before transferring to a wire rack to cool completely. For bread, allowing it to cool completely before slicing helps set the structure and enhances the flavor.

Underestimating the importance of ingredient quality can also lead to subpar results. Using fresh, high-quality ingredients can make a significant difference in the taste and texture of your baked goods. For instance, using real butter instead of margarine, fresh eggs, and high-quality chocolate can elevate your baking. Additionally, ingredients like vanilla extract and spices lose their potency over time, so replacing them regularly ensures your baked goods have the best possible flavor.

Lastly, not keeping a baking journal is a missed opportunity for improvement. Documenting your baking experiences, including any adjustments made, how the dough or batter behaved, and the final results, can help you learn from your mistakes and successes. Over time, this journal becomes a valuable resource, helping you refine your techniques and achieve consistently excellent results.

In conclusion, avoiding common baking mistakes involves a combination of preparation, attention to detail, and understanding the science behind baking. By thoroughly reading recipes, accurately measuring ingredients, controlling temperatures, and following proper techniques, you can enhance your baking skills and enjoy consistently delicious results. Embracing these practices not only prevents errors but also builds a solid foundation for exploring more advanced baking endeavors with confidence. A crucial aspect of baking is understanding the importance of patience. Rushing through steps or not allowing sufficient time for processes like proofing, resting, or cooling can result in disappointing outcomes. For instance, bread dough needs time to rise and develop its structure and flavor. Skipping or shortening this step can lead to dense, underdeveloped loaves. Similarly, resting cookie dough in the refrigerator allows the flavors to meld and the fat to solidify, resulting in cookies that spread less and have a better texture. Patience is also key when it comes to cooling baked goods. Cutting into a hot cake or bread can cause it to crumble or lose its moisture. Allowing it to cool completely ensures that the structure sets properly and the flavors are at their best.

Essential Baking Tools and Equipment

Baking, at its core, is a harmonious blend of science and art, requiring precise measurements and techniques to create delicious treats. However, the tools and equipment you use can significantly impact your baking experience and results. Investing in quality essentials can streamline the process, ensure accuracy, and enhance the overall quality of your baked goods. This chapter delves into the must-have baking tools and equipment that every baker, from beginners to seasoned professionals, should have in their kitchen arsenal.

A solid foundation for any baker starts with a set of reliable measuring tools. Accurate measurements are crucial in baking, where even slight deviations can alter the final product. Dry measuring cups are essential for ingredients like flour and sugar, while liquid measuring cups, typically made of clear plastic or glass, are designed for ingredients like milk, oil, and water. Measuring spoons are indispensable for smaller quantities of ingredients such as baking powder, salt, and vanilla extract. To ensure precision, it's advisable to invest in a kitchen scale. This tool allows you to measure ingredients by weight, providing greater accuracy than volume measurements, particularly for ingredients like flour, which can vary in density.

Mixing bowls are another fundamental component of a well-equipped kitchen. A variety of sizes is beneficial, as different recipes require different capacities. Stainless steel mixing bowls are durable, versatile, and often come with non-slip bases, making them ideal for vigorous mixing. Glass bowls are also useful as they are microwave-safe and allow you to see the ingredients as you mix. Silicone bowls, known for their flexibility, are excellent for melting ingredients like chocolate, as they can be easily manipulated to pour contents without spilling.

When it comes to combining ingredients, having the right mixing tools is essential. A sturdy whisk is indispensable for tasks like beating eggs, whipping cream, and mixing dry ingredients. Wooden spoons are great for stirring thick batters and doughs, offering the strength needed for tougher mixing jobs. Silicone spatulas are heat-resistant and perfect for scraping bowls, folding ingredients, and smoothing batters. These spatulas are also invaluable for ensuring that every last bit of batter is transferred from the bowl to the baking pan, minimizing waste.

Electric mixers, both handheld and stand mixers, can significantly ease the mixing process. Handheld mixers are lightweight, portable, and ideal for smaller tasks like whipping cream or mixing cake batter. Stand mixers, while more of an investment, offer hands-free mixing and come with various attachments for tasks like kneading dough, whipping egg whites, and more. A stand mixer can be a game-changer, providing consistent results and saving time and effort, especially for recipes that require prolonged mixing or kneading.

Baking pans and sheets are the canvases for your baked creations. A variety of sizes and shapes ensures you can tackle any recipe with confidence. Round cake pans, typically 8 or 9 inches in diameter, are essential for layer cakes. Rectangular baking dishes, like a 9x13-inch pan, are versatile for cakes, brownies, and casseroles. Muffin tins, available in standard and mini sizes, are perfect for cupcakes, muffins, and even savory dishes like quiches. Cookie sheets or baking trays, preferably with a non-stick surface or lined with silicone mats, ensure even baking and easy release of cookies and other baked goods. For bread enthusiasts, loaf pans and a Dutch oven are indispensable. Loaf pans are ideal for sandwich bread, quick bread, and pound cakes, while a Dutch oven is perfect for artisanal bread that requires high heat and steam.

Rolling pins are a must for tasks like rolling out dough for cookies, pie crusts, and pastries. Wooden rolling pins are traditional and effective, while silicone or marble rolling pins can offer non-stick properties and ease of cleaning. Having a rolling pin with adjustable thickness rings can help ensure your dough is rolled out evenly, which is crucial for consistent baking results.

Pastry brushes, often overlooked, are vital for applying glazes, egg washes, and melted butter. Silicone brushes are preferred for their durability and ease of cleaning, as they don't shed bristles like traditional brushes. A bench scraper is another versatile tool, useful for cutting dough, transferring ingredients, and cleaning work surfaces. Its flat, broad blade makes it easy to portion dough evenly and ensures a clean workspace.

For those who enjoy detailed decorating, a set of piping bags and tips is essential. Reusable silicone piping bags are eco-friendly and durable, while disposable plastic bags offer convenience for quick cleanup. Various piping tips allow you to create intricate designs with frosting, from simple borders to elaborate flowers. Couplers, which hold the tips in place, make it easy to switch tips without changing the bag, offering flexibility and creativity in your decorating.

Thermometers, both oven and instant-read, are crucial for accurate baking. An oven thermometer ensures your oven is at the correct temperature, as many home ovens are not perfectly calibrated. An instant-read thermometer is invaluable for checking the internal temperature of bread, cakes, and meat, ensuring they are cooked to perfection without overbaking or undercooking. For candy and caramel making, a candy thermometer is indispensable, providing precise temperature readings required for these delicate processes.

Cooling racks are essential for allowing air to circulate around baked goods, ensuring they cool evenly and preventing sogginess. Wire racks elevate your cookies, cakes, and bread off the baking surface, promoting faster cooling and preserving texture. Stacking cooling racks are a great space-saving solution, especially when baking large batches.

Baking mats and parchment paper are valuable for non-stick baking and easy cleanup. Silicone baking mats are reusable, durable, and provide a perfect non-stick surface for cookies, macarons, and other delicate baked goods. Parchment paper, available in rolls or pre-cut sheets, is versatile for lining cake pans, wrapping dough, and even making pastry cones for decorating.

Investing in a quality sifter or fine-mesh sieve is essential for tasks like sifting flour, cocoa powder, and powdered sugar. Sifting aerates these ingredients, removes lumps, and ensures an even distribution in your batter or dough, contributing to a lighter, more uniform texture. A fine-mesh sieve can also be used for dusting powdered sugar over finished baked goods, adding a professional touch to your presentation.

Having a set of quality knives is crucial for tasks like chopping nuts, slicing fruit, and cutting dough. A chef's knife is versatile for a variety of tasks, while a serrated knife is ideal for slicing bread and delicate items like tomatoes or cakes. A paring knife is perfect for smaller, detailed work, such as peeling fruit or trimming pastry.

Finally, a well-organized kitchen is key to a smooth baking experience. Keeping your tools and equipment neatly stored and easily accessible can save time and reduce stress. Drawer organizers for measuring spoons, spatulas, and whisks, and dedicated storage for larger items like mixing bowls and baking pans, help maintain an efficient workspace. Labeling containers for ingredients and tools can further streamline your process, ensuring you can quickly find what you need when you need it.

While the initial investment in quality baking tools and equipment may seem significant, the benefits far outweigh the costs. These tools not only enhance your baking efficiency and precision but also contribute to better results and a more enjoyable baking experience. By equipping your kitchen with these essentials, you set yourself up for success, enabling you to tackle any recipe with confidence and creativity. A well-stocked kitchen also includes a few specialty tools that, while not strictly necessary for every baker, can elevate your baking game and expand your repertoire. These tools allow you to explore more advanced techniques and recipes, adding an extra layer of fun and creativity to your baking endeavors.

Chapter 3

Quick Breads and Muffins

Classic Banana Bread

Banana bread, a beloved staple in many households, offers a comforting blend of sweetness and warmth that can make any kitchen feel like home. This classic treat, with its moist crumb and rich banana flavor, is a testament to the transformative power of simple ingredients. In this chapter, we'll explore the nuances of baking the perfect banana bread, from selecting the right bananas to mastering the baking process.

The foundation of any great banana bread lies in its main ingredient: bananas. Overripe bananas, with their spotted and slightly blackened skins, are ideal for this recipe. These bananas are not only sweeter but also softer, making them easier to mash and incorporate into the batter. The natural sugars that develop as bananas ripen add depth to the flavor, ensuring a rich and aromatic loaf. If your bananas are not quite ripe enough, you can speed up the process by placing them in a brown paper bag for a day or two.

Once you have your bananas ready, the next step is to gather your ingredients. Classic banana bread recipes typically call for flour, sugar, eggs, butter, baking soda, salt, and vanilla extract. Each ingredient plays a crucial role in the final product. Flour provides structure, sugar adds sweetness, eggs contribute to the bread's richness and moisture, and butter offers a tender crumb. Baking soda acts as a leavening agent, helping the bread rise, while salt enhances the overall flavor. Vanilla extract, though optional, adds a lovely aromatic note that complements the bananas.

To create the batter, start by preheating your oven to 350°F (175°C) and greasing a loaf pan. Cream the butter and sugar together in a large mixing bowl until the mixture is light and fluffy. This step is essential as it incorporates air into the batter, contributing to a lighter texture. Next, add the eggs one at a time, beating well after each addition. Incorporating the eggs gradually ensures a smooth and cohesive batter.

In a separate bowl, combine the flour, baking soda, and salt. Mixing the dry ingredients separately helps distribute the leavening agent evenly throughout the batter, preventing any unpleasant pockets of baking soda. Gradually add the dry ingredients to the wet mixture, stirring just until combined. Overmixing can lead to a dense and tough bread, so it's important to mix only until no streaks of flour remain.

Mash the bananas thoroughly and fold them into the batter along with the vanilla extract. The consistency of the mashed bananas can vary depending on your preference. Some bakers prefer a smoother mash for a more uniform texture, while others enjoy a chunkier mash for added bursts of banana flavor in each bite. Once the bananas and vanilla are incorporated, pour the batter into the prepared loaf pan.

Baking banana bread requires patience and attention to detail. Place the loaf pan in the preheated oven and bake for about 60 minutes, or until a toothpick inserted into the center comes out clean. Baking times can vary based on your oven and the specific loaf pan you use, so it's crucial to keep an eye on the bread as it bakes. The top should be golden brown and slightly domed, with a crack running down the center.

Allow the banana bread to cool in the pan for about 10 minutes before transferring it to a wire rack to cool completely. This step is vital as it allows the bread to set and prevents it from becoming soggy. Cooling on a wire rack ensures that air circulates around the loaf, maintaining its texture.

While the classic banana bread recipe is delightful on its own, there are countless variations to explore. Adding mix-ins like chocolate chips, chopped nuts, or dried fruit can elevate the flavor and texture of your banana bread. Walnuts or pecans add a satisfying crunch, while chocolate chips introduce a rich, indulgent element. For a tropical twist, consider incorporating shredded coconut or diced pineapple.

Spices can also enhance the flavor profile of your banana bread. A teaspoon of cinnamon or a pinch of nutmeg can add warmth and complexity, complementing the sweetness of the bananas. For a more adventurous twist, try adding a bit of cardamom or allspice.

If you're looking to make your banana bread a bit healthier, there are several substitutions you can make without sacrificing flavor. Whole wheat flour can replace some or all of the all-purpose flour, adding a nutty flavor and extra fiber. Honey or maple syrup can be used in place of granulated sugar for a natural sweetness. Greek yogurt or applesauce can substitute for butter, reducing the fat content while keeping the bread moist and tender.

For those with dietary restrictions, banana bread can easily be adapted to be gluten-free or vegan. Gluten-free flour blends work well as a direct substitute for all-purpose flour. For a vegan version, flaxseed meal mixed with water can replace eggs, and plant-based butter or oil can be used instead of dairy butter. These adjustments allow everyone to enjoy this classic treat, regardless of dietary needs.

Storage is an important consideration for banana bread, as it tends to dry out if not properly kept. Once completely cooled, wrap the loaf tightly in plastic wrap or aluminum foil and store it at room temperature for up to three days. For longer storage, banana bread can be frozen. Slice the loaf and wrap each piece individually in plastic wrap, then place the slices in a resealable freezer bag. Frozen banana bread can last for up to three months and can be thawed at room temperature or warmed in the oven.

Banana bread's versatility extends beyond being a simple snack or breakfast item. It can be transformed into a delightful dessert by serving it with a scoop of vanilla ice cream or a dollop of whipped cream. Toasting slices and spreading them with butter or cream cheese can also make for a delicious and comforting treat. For a special brunch, consider making banana bread French toast by dipping slices in an egg mixture and frying them until golden brown.

The story of banana bread is one of resilience and creativity. It gained popularity during the Great Depression when resourceful homemakers sought ways to use overripe bananas that would otherwise go to waste. This spirit of ingenuity continues today, as bakers around the world put their own unique spins on this timeless recipe. Whether you're a seasoned baker or a novice in the kitchen, banana bread offers a rewarding and comforting baking experience.

In the end, the joy of baking banana bread lies not only in the delicious results but also in the process itself. The aroma that fills your kitchen as the bread bakes, the satisfaction of slicing into a perfectly moist loaf, and the pleasure of sharing it with loved ones all contribute to its enduring appeal. By mastering the basics and experimenting with variations, you can make banana bread a cherished part of your baking repertoire. Banana bread also serves as a wonderful canvas for creativity. Beyond traditional ingredients and methods, there are innovative techniques and elements you can introduce to make your banana bread uniquely yours. For instance, incorporating a swirl of Nutella or peanut butter into the batter before baking can create delightful pockets of flavor. Simply dollop your chosen spread over the batter and use a knife to create a marbled effect. This not only enhances the taste but also adds a visually appealing twist to the classic loaf.

Zucchini Bread Variations

Zucchini bread is a delightful way to use the bountiful harvest from your summer garden, turning a humble vegetable into a moist and flavorful treat. What makes zucchini bread so appealing is its versatility; it can be sweet or savory, simple or elaborate, and it pairs well with a variety of ingredients. This chapter will guide you through several zucchini bread variations, ensuring you have a repertoire of recipes to suit any occasion or preference.

The foundation of any great zucchini bread is, of course, the zucchini. Fresh, medium-sized zucchinis are ideal, as they are tender and have a balanced flavor. Larger zucchinis can be used, but they tend to be more fibrous and contain more water, which may affect the bread's texture. Begin by washing the zucchini thoroughly and trimming the ends. Grate the zucchini using a box grater or a food processor. Depending on the recipe, you may need to squeeze out excess moisture using a clean kitchen towel or cheesecloth, especially if your batter seems too wet.

A basic zucchini bread recipe typically includes flour, sugar, eggs, oil, baking soda, baking powder, salt, and spices such as cinnamon or nutmeg. The zucchini adds moisture and a subtle flavor, while the spices enhance the overall taste. To prepare the batter, start by preheating your oven to 350°F (175°C) and greasing a loaf pan. In a large mixing bowl, whisk together the dry ingredients. In a separate bowl, beat the eggs and mix in the oil and sugar until well combined. Add the grated zucchini and mix thoroughly. Gradually incorporate the dry ingredients into the wet mixture, stirring just until combined. Pour the batter into the prepared loaf pan and bake for about 60 minutes, or until a toothpick inserted into the center comes out clean. Let the bread cool in the pan for 10 minutes before transferring it to a wire rack to cool completely.

While the basic recipe is delicious on its own, experimenting with different flavors and add-ins can take your zucchini bread to the next level. One popular variation is to incorporate chocolate. Adding cocoa powder to the dry ingredients and folding in chocolate chips creates a rich, chocolatey loaf that will satisfy any sweet tooth. For a more indulgent version, try adding a swirl of cream cheese filling. Simply mix softened cream cheese with a bit of sugar and vanilla extract, and swirl it into the batter before baking.

Nuts and dried fruits are also excellent additions to zucchini bread. Walnuts, pecans, or almonds add a delightful crunch and complement the bread's moist texture. Dried cranberries, raisins, or chopped dates provide a burst of sweetness and chewy texture. To prevent dried fruits from sinking to the bottom of the loaf, toss them in a little flour before folding them into the batter.

For a healthier twist, you can substitute part or all of the all-purpose flour with whole wheat flour or a gluten-free flour blend. Whole wheat flour adds a nutty flavor and additional fiber, while gluten-free flour ensures that those with dietary restrictions can enjoy this tasty treat. Honey or maple syrup can replace granulated sugar, adding natural sweetness and depth of flavor. Additionally, using Greek yogurt or applesauce instead of oil can reduce the fat content while maintaining the bread's moistness.

Savory zucchini bread is another exciting variation. Omit the sugar and spices, and instead add ingredients like grated cheese, chopped herbs, and sautéed onions or garlic. A combination of sharp cheddar, fresh thyme, and caramelized onions makes for a delicious loaf that pairs well with soups and salads. For a Mediterranean twist, try adding crumbled feta cheese, chopped olives, and dried oregano.

Another creative variation is to make zucchini muffins instead of a loaf. Muffins are perfect for portion control and make a convenient on-the-go snack. The batter can be spooned into a greased muffin tin and baked at 350°F (175°C) for 20-25 minutes, or until a toothpick inserted into the center comes out clean. This approach also allows for experimentation with different mix-ins and toppings. For example, you could sprinkle the tops with a streusel made from oats, brown sugar, and butter, or add a dollop of nut butter to the center of each muffin before baking.

Zucchini bread can also be made more nutritious by adding grated carrots, mashed bananas, or pumpkin puree. These ingredients not only enhance the flavor but also increase the nutritional value of the bread. Carrots add sweetness and a lovely orange hue, bananas contribute natural sweetness and moisture, and pumpkin puree provides a rich, earthy flavor.

For a more adventurous take, consider incorporating spices from around the world. Adding a teaspoon of ground ginger and a pinch of cloves can give your zucchini bread a warm, spiced flavor reminiscent of gingerbread. Cardamom and a touch of saffron can add an exotic, aromatic twist. Experimenting with different spice blends allows you to tailor the bread to your personal taste and explore new culinary horizons.

Presentation is another way to elevate your zucchini bread. Drizzling a simple glaze made from powdered sugar and lemon juice over the top of a cooled loaf adds a touch of elegance and a burst of citrus flavor. Alternatively, you can dust the top with powdered sugar for a classic look, or spread a thin layer of cream cheese frosting for a decadent finish.

Storage and serving suggestions are important to consider as well. Zucchini bread can be stored at room temperature for up to three days, wrapped tightly in plastic wrap or aluminum foil. For longer storage, it can be frozen. Wrap the cooled loaf or muffins in plastic wrap and place them in a resealable freezer bag. Frozen zucchini bread can last for up to three months and can be thawed at room temperature or warmed in the oven.

Zucchini bread is not only a delicious treat but also a wonderful way to introduce vegetables into your diet in a fun and accessible form. It can be enjoyed at breakfast, as a snack, or even as a dessert, making it a versatile addition to any meal plan. The process of baking zucchini bread is also a great opportunity to involve children in the kitchen. They can help with grating the zucchini, mixing the batter, and even coming up with their own creative variations.

In conclusion, zucchini bread is a versatile and delightful baked good that can be customized to suit any taste or occasion. Whether you prefer it sweet or savory, simple or elaborate, there is a zucchini bread variation for everyone. By experimenting with different ingredients and techniques, you can create a unique and delicious loaf that reflects your personal style and culinary creativity. The joy of baking and sharing zucchini bread lies not only in the delicious results but also in the process of creating something special and sharing it with others. Zucchini bread also offers an excellent opportunity to explore the concept of seasonal eating. During the summer months, when zucchinis are in abundance, making zucchini bread is a wonderful way to use up the excess produce. However, it can also be adapted to incorporate other seasonal ingredients, ensuring that your baking is always fresh and relevant to the time of year.

Perfect Blueberry Muffins

Blueberry muffins are a beloved classic, offering a burst of fruity sweetness in every bite. The secret to perfect blueberry muffins lies in the balance of ingredients, the technique used to combine them, and the quality of the blueberries themselves. This chapter will guide you through the steps to create blueberry muffins that are tender, moist, and packed with flavor, while also exploring variations that can elevate this simple treat.

Start with the blueberries. Fresh is best, but frozen blueberries can also be used if fresh ones are out of season. When using frozen blueberries, do not thaw them before adding to the batter, as this can cause them to bleed and turn the batter purple. Select plump, firm blueberries for the best results, and gently rinse and dry them if they are fresh. Tossing the blueberries in a tablespoon of flour before folding them into the batter helps to distribute them evenly and prevents them from sinking to the bottom during baking.

A key component to perfect blueberry muffins is the batter. Begin by preheating your oven to 375°F (190°C) and lining a muffin tin with paper liners or greasing it well. In a large bowl, whisk together the dry ingredients: 2 cups of all-purpose flour, 1 cup of granulated sugar, 2 teaspoons of baking powder, and 1/2 teaspoon of salt. In a separate bowl, combine the wet ingredients: 2 large eggs, 1/2 cup of milk, 1/2 cup of vegetable oil or melted butter, and 1 teaspoon of vanilla extract. Mix the wet ingredients until well combined.

To avoid overmixing, which can result in tough muffins, gently fold the wet ingredients into the dry ingredients using a spatula. The batter should be lumpy and slightly thick. Carefully fold in the flour-coated blueberries until they are just distributed throughout the batter. This minimal stirring ensures that the muffins remain tender and light.

Fill each muffin cup about three-quarters full with batter. This allows room for the muffins to rise without overflowing. For a bakery-style touch, sprinkle the tops with a mixture of coarse sugar and a pinch of cinnamon. This adds a delightful crunch and a hint of spice to each bite.

Bake the muffins for 20-25 minutes, or until a toothpick inserted into the center of a muffin comes out clean or with just a few moist crumbs. The tops should be golden brown and slightly domed. Allow the muffins to cool in the pan for 5 minutes before transferring them to a wire rack to cool completely. This short cooling period helps the muffins set and makes them easier to remove from the pan.

One of the joys of baking blueberry muffins is experimenting with variations to suit different tastes and occasions. For a healthier version, consider using whole wheat flour or a blend of whole wheat and all-purpose flour. This adds a nutty flavor and boosts the fiber content. You can also substitute part of the granulated sugar with honey or maple syrup for a natural sweetness.

Adding lemon zest and a tablespoon of lemon juice to the batter creates a bright, citrusy flavor that pairs beautifully with the blueberries. The acidity of the lemon enhances the blueberries' natural sweetness and adds a refreshing twist. For an extra touch, drizzle the cooled muffins with a simple lemon glaze made from powdered sugar and lemon juice.

Another delicious variation is to incorporate a streusel topping. To make the streusel, combine 1/2 cup of flour, 1/2 cup of brown sugar, 1/4 cup of melted butter, and a pinch of cinnamon until the mixture resembles coarse crumbs. Sprinkle a generous amount of streusel over each muffin before baking. The result is a delightful contrast of textures with a crunchy, sweet topping complementing the soft, moist muffin.

For those who enjoy a bit of indulgence, adding a cream cheese filling can take your blueberry muffins to the next level. To prepare the filling, beat together 4 ounces of softened cream cheese, 1/4 cup of granulated sugar, and 1 teaspoon of vanilla extract until smooth. Spoon a small amount of batter into each muffin cup, add a dollop of the cream cheese mixture, and then top with more batter. This creates a luscious, creamy center that surprises and delights with every bite.

Including additional fruits and nuts can also enhance the flavor and texture of blueberry muffins. Chopped nuts like walnuts or pecans add a satisfying crunch, while shredded coconut provides a tropical twist. Combining blueberries with other berries, such as raspberries or blackberries, adds complexity and a burst of color. These variations allow for endless customization based on personal preferences and seasonal availability.

For a more decadent treat, consider making blueberry muffin bread pudding. Cube leftover muffins and place them in a baking dish. Whisk together eggs, milk, sugar, and vanilla, and pour the mixture over the muffin cubes. Allow the bread pudding to soak for 30 minutes before baking at 350°F (175°C) until golden and set. This transforms day-old muffins into a rich, comforting dessert.

Presentation can also enhance the enjoyment of blueberry muffins. Baking them in decorative paper liners or using a decorative muffin tin adds a touch of elegance. For special occasions, such as brunches or afternoon teas, arranging the muffins on a tiered cake stand creates an inviting display. Garnishing with a dusting of powdered sugar or a drizzle of glaze adds visual appeal and a hint of extra sweetness.

Storing blueberry muffins properly ensures they stay fresh and delicious. Once cooled, store them in an airtight container at room temperature for up to three days. For longer storage, muffins can be frozen. Wrap each muffin individually in plastic wrap and place them in a resealable freezer bag. They can be frozen for up to three months and thawed at room temperature or warmed in the oven before serving.

Blueberry muffins are not only a delightful treat but also a wonderful way to bring people together. Baking a batch to share with family and friends creates moments of connection and joy. Whether enjoyed with a cup of coffee in the morning or as an afternoon snack, blueberry muffins are a versatile and comforting addition to any occasion.

Involving children in the baking process can also be a rewarding experience. They can help with measuring ingredients, mixing the batter, and even placing the blueberries in the muffin cups. This not only teaches them valuable skills but also fosters a love of baking and an appreciation for homemade treats.

Perfect blueberry muffins are within reach when you pay attention to the quality of the ingredients, the balance of flavors, and the baking techniques used. By experimenting with different variations and personal touches, you can create muffins that are uniquely yours. The joy of baking and sharing blueberry muffins lies not only in the delicious results but also in the process of creating something special and sharing it with others. For those seeking to elevate their blueberry muffins with a touch of sophistication, consider experimenting with flavor infusions and gourmet ingredients. Infusing the batter with herbs and spices can add a subtle, complex flavor profile that surprises and delights the palate. For instance, adding a teaspoon of finely chopped fresh thyme or rosemary to the batter can create an unexpected yet harmonious blend with the sweetness of the blueberries. Similarly, incorporating a pinch of cardamom or nutmeg can introduce a warm, aromatic note that enhances the overall taste.

Savory Cheese and Herb Muffins

Savory cheese and herb muffins are an excellent alternative to their sweet counterparts, offering a delightful combination of flavors that can complement a variety of meals. These muffins can be served as an accompaniment to soups and salads, as a snack on their own, or even as part of a hearty breakfast. The key to making perfect savory cheese and herb muffins lies in the balance of cheese, herbs, and other ingredients, as well as the technique used to combine them.

To start, preheat your oven to 375°F (190°C) and prepare a muffin tin by lining it with paper liners or greasing it well. The choice of cheese is crucial to achieving the desired flavor and texture. Sharp cheddar is a popular option because it melts well and provides a robust flavor. However, you can experiment with other cheeses such as Gruyère for a nutty taste, feta for a tangy kick, or even a combination of cheeses to add complexity.

In a large bowl, whisk together the dry ingredients: 2 cups of all-purpose flour, 1 tablespoon of baking powder, 1 teaspoon of salt, and 1 teaspoon of sugar. The sugar, although minimal, helps to balance the flavors and promote browning. To this dry mixture, add 1 cup of grated cheese, making sure to coat the cheese with the flour mixture to ensure even distribution throughout the batter.

The choice of herbs can greatly influence the flavor profile of the muffins. Fresh herbs are preferred for their vibrant flavor and aroma. A classic combination is 1 tablespoon each of chopped fresh chives, parsley, and dill. However, you can tailor the herbs to your taste or what you have on hand. Rosemary and thyme, for example, add a more earthy and robust flavor, while basil and oregano can give an Italian twist. If using dried herbs, reduce the quantity to about 1 teaspoon each, as dried herbs are more concentrated in flavor.

In a separate bowl, whisk together the wet ingredients: 2 large eggs, 1 cup of buttermilk, and 1/2 cup of melted butter or vegetable oil. Buttermilk is preferred for its slight tanginess and ability to tenderize the batter, but regular milk can be used if that's what you have. The fat content in the butter or oil is essential for creating a moist texture.

Gently fold the wet ingredients into the dry ingredients using a spatula, being careful not to overmix. The batter should be thick and lumpy, which helps to keep the muffins tender. Overmixing can lead to dense, tough muffins. Scoop the batter into the prepared muffin tin, filling each cup about three-quarters full. This allows room for the muffins to rise without overflowing.

For an added layer of flavor and texture, consider sprinkling the tops with additional cheese and a few extra chopped herbs before baking. This not only enhances the visual appeal but also creates a deliciously crispy top.

Bake the muffins for 20-25 minutes, or until a toothpick inserted into the center of a muffin comes out clean or with just a few moist crumbs. The tops should be golden brown and slightly domed. Allow the muffins to cool in the pan for 5 minutes before transferring them to a wire rack to cool completely. This brief cooling period helps the muffins set and makes them easier to remove from the pan.

Savory cheese and herb muffins are incredibly versatile and can be customized to suit different tastes and dietary needs. For a healthier version, consider using whole wheat flour or a blend of whole wheat and all-purpose flour. This adds a nutty flavor and boosts the fiber content. You can also incorporate vegetables such as finely chopped bell peppers, spinach, or sun-dried tomatoes to add color and nutritional value.

Adding a protein such as cooked bacon, ham, or sautéed mushrooms can turn these muffins into a more substantial snack or meal. Simply fold in about 1 cup of your chosen add-in along with the cheese and herbs. This makes the muffins heartier and more filling, perfect for a grab-and-go breakfast or a satisfying snack.

For a touch of spice, consider adding a pinch of cayenne pepper or some finely chopped jalapeños to the batter. This gives the muffins a bit of a kick and pairs well with the richness of the cheese. Alternatively, a teaspoon of mustard powder can add a subtle depth of flavor that complements the sharpness of the cheddar.

If you are looking to make these muffins gluten-free, substitute the all-purpose flour with a gluten-free flour blend. Ensure that the baking powder and other ingredients are also gluten-free. The texture may vary slightly, but the muffins should still be delicious and satisfying.

Presentation is important, especially if you are serving these muffins for a special occasion or as part of a spread. Baking the muffins in decorative paper liners or using a decorative muffin tin can add a touch of elegance. For a rustic look, consider baking the muffins directly in a cast-iron skillet or mini loaf pans. This not only looks charming but also creates a wonderful crust.

Storing savory cheese and herb muffins properly ensures they stay fresh and delicious. Once cooled, store them in an airtight container at room temperature for up to three days. For longer storage, muffins can be frozen. Wrap each muffin individually in plastic wrap and place them in a resealable freezer bag. They can be frozen for up to three months and thawed at room temperature or warmed in the oven before serving.

Savory muffins are not only delicious but also a wonderful way to bring people together. Baking a batch to share with family and friends creates moments of connection and joy. Whether enjoyed as part of a meal or as a standalone snack, savory cheese and herb muffins are a versatile and comforting addition to any table.

Involving children in the baking process can also be a rewarding experience. They can help with measuring ingredients, mixing the batter, and even sprinkling the cheese and herbs. This not only teaches them valuable skills but also fosters a love of baking and an appreciation for homemade treats.

Perfect savory cheese and herb muffins are within reach when you pay attention to the quality of the ingredients, the balance of flavors, and the baking techniques used. By experimenting with different variations and personal touches, you can create muffins that are uniquely yours. The joy of baking and sharing savory muffins lies not only in the delicious results but also in the process of creating something special and sharing it with others.

For a final touch, consider serving the muffins warm with a pat of butter or a dollop of sour cream. Pairing the muffins with a bowl of soup or a fresh salad can turn a simple meal into a delightful experience. Whether you are baking for a casual family dinner or a special occasion, savory cheese and herb muffins are sure to impress and satisfy. The flexibility of savory cheese and herb muffins also extends to their role in various culinary themes and traditions. For instance, incorporating regional cheeses and herbs can lend a unique cultural twist to your muffins. Imagine using Manchego cheese and smoked paprika for a Spanish-inspired muffin, or perhaps a combination of Parmesan and basil for an Italian touch. Exploring these variations not only expands your culinary repertoire but also offers a delightful way to experience global flavors in a familiar format.

Gluten-Free Quick Breads

Gluten-free quick breads have surged in popularity as more people become aware of gluten sensitivities and celiac disease. These breads, which do not require yeast or lengthy rising times, offer a convenient and delicious alternative to traditional wheat-based varieties. The challenge lies in achieving the right texture and flavor without gluten, but with the right ingredients and techniques, it is entirely possible to bake quick breads that are both satisfying and delectable.

The foundation of a successful gluten-free quick bread starts with selecting the appropriate flour blend. Unlike wheat flour, which contains gluten that provides structure and elasticity, gluten-free flours need to be combined to mimic these properties. A typical gluten-free flour blend might include rice flour for a light texture, tapioca starch for chewiness, and potato starch for moisture retention. Many home bakers find that using a commercially available gluten-free all-purpose flour blend simplifies the process, as these blends are formulated to balance taste and performance.

Once you have your flour blend, it's essential to incorporate a binding agent to help provide structure. Commonly used binders include xanthan gum or guar gum, which are added in small amounts (usually about 1 teaspoon per cup of flour). These gums help trap air and moisture, creating a texture more akin to that of traditional breads.

To begin, preheat your oven to 350°F (175°C) and prepare your baking pan by greasing it lightly or lining it with parchment paper. In a large mixing bowl, combine 2 cups of your gluten-free flour blend with 1 teaspoon of xanthan gum (if not already included in your flour blend), 1 tablespoon of baking powder, 1/2 teaspoon of baking soda, and 1/2 teaspoon of salt. These dry ingredients form the base of your bread, ensuring it rises properly and has a balanced flavor.

In a separate bowl, whisk together the wet ingredients: 2 large eggs, 1 cup of buttermilk (or a dairy-free alternative such as almond milk with 1 tablespoon of vinegar), 1/3 cup of vegetable oil, and 1/2 cup of sugar. The buttermilk not only adds moisture but also helps to tenderize the crumb. If you prefer a lower sugar option, honey or maple syrup can be used as natural sweeteners.

Gently combine the wet and dry ingredients, mixing just until incorporated. Overmixing can lead to a dense and tough bread, so it's important to stop as soon as the batter comes together. At this stage, you can add any flavorings or mix-ins you desire. Popular choices include mashed bananas for a classic banana bread, shredded zucchini for a moist and nutritious loaf, or a combination of blueberries and lemon zest for a refreshing burst of flavor.

Pour the batter into your prepared pan, smoothing the top with a spatula. To add a bit of visual appeal and extra flavor, you can sprinkle the top with nuts, seeds, or a dusting of cinnamon sugar. Bake in the preheated oven for 45-55 minutes, or until a toothpick inserted into the center comes out clean. The baking time may vary slightly depending on the moisture content of your mix-ins and the specific characteristics of your oven.

Allow the bread to cool in the pan for about 10 minutes before transferring it to a wire rack to cool completely. This cooling period is crucial as it allows the bread to set and makes it easier to slice without crumbling. Once cooled, gluten-free quick bread can be stored at room temperature in an airtight container for up to three days, or frozen for longer storage. To freeze, wrap the bread tightly in plastic wrap and place it in a resealable freezer bag.

Exploring different flavor combinations and add-ins can make gluten-free quick breads a versatile staple in your baking repertoire. For a savory option, try incorporating grated cheese, chopped herbs, and a pinch of garlic powder into the batter. This can create a delightful cheese and herb bread that pairs well with soups and salads. Alternatively, adding dried fruits and nuts can transform your loaf into a hearty breakfast or snack option.

Experimenting with different gluten-free flours can also yield unique and delicious results. For instance, using almond flour can add a rich, nutty flavor and extra moisture, while coconut flour, with its high fiber content, can create a denser, more filling bread. When using these flours, it's important to note their distinct characteristics—coconut flour, for example, absorbs much more liquid than other flours, so you'll need to adjust the liquid ratios accordingly.

For those who are new to gluten-free baking, it's helpful to keep in mind that gluten-free batters often have a different consistency than their gluten-containing counterparts. They may appear thicker or more sticky, but resist the urge to add more liquid unless absolutely necessary. Trust the process and the recipe, and you'll likely find that the final product is just right.

Involving children in the baking process can be a wonderful way to introduce them to the joys of gluten-free baking. They can help measure ingredients, mix the batter, and, of course, enjoy the delicious results.

This not only teaches valuable kitchen skills but also fosters an appreciation for homemade, gluten-free treats.

Gluten-free quick breads can also be a thoughtful gift for friends and family, especially those who follow a gluten-free diet. Baking a loaf for a loved one not only shows you care but also provides them with a tasty, homemade treat that they can enjoy without worry. Packaging the bread in a decorative loaf pan or wrapping it in a festive cloth can add a personal touch that enhances the gift.

Beyond just baking for special occasions, gluten-free quick breads can be incorporated into your regular meal planning. They make excellent accompaniments to breakfasts, lunches, and dinners, and can easily be made ahead of time and stored for convenience. Slicing and freezing individual portions allows for quick and easy access to a delicious slice of bread whenever you need it.

For those looking to reduce their sugar intake, there are plenty of ways to make gluten-free quick breads healthier without sacrificing flavor. Using unsweetened applesauce or mashed ripe bananas can add natural sweetness and moisture, reducing the need for added sugars. Additionally, incorporating whole ingredients such as oats, flaxseeds, and chia seeds can boost the nutritional value, adding fiber, protein, and healthy fats.

Embracing gluten-free quick breads opens up a world of culinary possibilities. With a bit of creativity and experimentation, you can develop a variety of delicious and satisfying breads that cater to different tastes and dietary needs. Whether you're baking for yourself, your family, or your friends, these breads offer a simple yet rewarding way to enjoy the pleasures of homemade baking.

The journey of mastering gluten-free quick breads is both educational and enjoyable. Each loaf you bake provides an opportunity to refine your skills, try new ingredients, and discover new favorite recipes. The satisfaction of pulling a perfectly baked loaf from the oven, knowing that it is both gluten-free and delicious, is a reward in itself. So, roll up your sleeves, gather your ingredients, and embark on the delightful adventure of gluten-free quick bread baking. As you delve deeper into the world of gluten-free quick breads, you may find yourself inspired to experiment with various cultural and seasonal influences. For instance, incorporating spices and ingredients typical of different cuisines can yield unique and memorable breads. Imagine a loaf infused with the warm spices of chai, featuring ginger, cardamom, and cinnamon, perfect for a cozy winter treat. Or perhaps a summer loaf bursting with tropical flavors like coconut, pineapple, and lime, offering a refreshing departure from more traditional flavors.

Chapter 4

Yeast Breads

Introduction to Yeast and Fermentation

Yeast and fermentation are the heartbeats of bread-making, transforming simple ingredients into flavorful, airy loaves. Understanding the science and art behind these processes can elevate your baking from basic to extraordinary. Yeast, a single-celled fungus, plays a crucial role in fermentation, a metabolic process that converts sugars into carbon dioxide and alcohol. This chapter delves into the intricacies of yeast and fermentation, providing you with the knowledge to harness their power in your baking endeavors.

Yeast comes in various forms, each with unique characteristics and uses. The most common types are active dry yeast, instant yeast, and fresh yeast. Active dry yeast is granulated and requires activation in warm water before use. Instant yeast, also known as rapid-rise or bread machine yeast, has finer grains and can be mixed directly with dry ingredients. Fresh yeast, sold in compressed cakes, is highly perishable but prized for its robust flavor and rapid activity.

Selecting the appropriate yeast for your baking project depends on factors such as recipe requirements, desired flavor, and convenience. Active dry yeast is a reliable choice for most bread recipes, providing a good balance of flavor and ease of use. Instant yeast is ideal for quick breads and recipes requiring fast rise times, while fresh yeast is often favored by professional bakers for its superior flavor and performance.

Fermentation begins when yeast is introduced to a mixture of flour and water, starting a complex biochemical process. Yeast feeds on the sugars present in the flour, producing carbon dioxide and alcohol as byproducts. The carbon dioxide gets trapped in the dough's gluten network, causing it to expand and rise. This fermentation process not only leavens the bread but also develops its flavor and texture.

Temperature plays a critical role in fermentation. Yeast is most active at temperatures between 75°F and 85°F (24°C to 29°C). Cooler temperatures slow down fermentation, leading to a longer rise time and a more complex flavor profile. Conversely, warmer temperatures speed up fermentation but can result in a less developed flavor. Finding the right balance is key to achieving the desired outcome.

Hydration levels, or the ratio of water to flour in the dough, also influence fermentation. Higher hydration doughs, which are wetter and more fluid, ferment more quickly and produce a more open crumb structure with larger holes. Lower hydration doughs, which are stiffer, ferment more slowly and result in a denser crumb. Adjusting hydration levels allows you to control the texture and appearance of your bread.

Salt is another important factor in fermentation. While it enhances flavor and strengthens gluten, it also regulates yeast activity. Adding salt directly to yeast can kill the organisms, so it's crucial to mix salt with the flour before combining it with the yeast or to add it after the initial mixing stage. Properly balancing salt ensures a controlled fermentation process and a well-seasoned bread.

Kneading the dough develops the gluten network, which is essential for trapping the carbon dioxide produced during fermentation. Gluten, a protein found in wheat, gives dough its elasticity and strength. By kneading, you align the gluten strands, creating a structure that can stretch and expand. Proper kneading results in a smooth, elastic dough that can rise effectively and hold its shape during baking.

The first rise, or bulk fermentation, is a critical phase where the dough develops flavor and structure. After mixing and kneading, the dough is left to rise until it doubles in size. This can take anywhere from 1 to 3 hours, depending on the yeast, temperature, and hydration. During this time, the yeast ferments the sugars, producing carbon dioxide and alcohol, which contribute to the bread's flavor and texture.

Punching down the dough after the first rise redistributes the yeast and sugars, releasing some of the carbon dioxide and preventing over-fermentation. This step also helps to even out the dough's temperature and prepare it for shaping. After punching down, the dough is shaped into its final form and left to rise again, known as the second rise or proofing.

Proofing allows the dough to reach its final volume before baking. This stage is typically shorter than the first rise, lasting 30 minutes to 1 hour. During proofing, the yeast continues to produce carbon dioxide, causing the dough to expand. Proper proofing ensures a light, airy crumb and a well-risen loaf. Under-proofing results in dense bread with a tight crumb, while over-proofing can cause the dough to collapse and lose its shape.

Scoring the dough before baking serves both functional and aesthetic purposes. By making shallow cuts on the surface of the dough, you control the direction in which it expands, preventing it from bursting unpredictably in the oven. Scoring also creates an attractive pattern on the crust, enhancing the bread's visual appeal. Use a sharp knife or a bread lame to make clean, precise cuts.

Baking transforms the fermented dough into bread, a process known as oven spring. The initial heat causes a rapid expansion of the carbon dioxide, resulting in a final burst of rising. As the temperature increases, the yeast dies, and the starches gelatinize, setting the bread's structure. The Maillard reaction, a chemical reaction between amino acids and reducing sugars, creates the bread's golden-brown crust and complex flavors.

Steam is vital during the initial stages of baking. It keeps the dough's surface moist, allowing it to expand fully before the crust sets. Professional bakers use steam-injected ovens, but you can achieve similar results at home by placing a pan of water in the oven or misting the dough with water before baking. Once the bread has expanded, the steam is removed, allowing the crust to form and develop its characteristic texture and color.

Cooling is the final step in the bread-making process. Freshly baked bread should be cooled on a wire rack to prevent the bottom from becoming soggy. Allowing the bread to cool completely before slicing ensures that the crumb sets properly and the flavors mature. Cutting into hot bread can result in a gummy texture and an uneven crumb.

Experimenting with different types of yeast and fermentation techniques can lead to exciting discoveries in your baking journey. Sourdough, for example, relies on wild yeast and lactic acid bacteria for fermentation, producing a tangy flavor and a chewy texture. By creating and maintaining a sourdough starter, you can explore the nuances of natural fermentation and develop a deeper understanding of the bread-making process.

Understanding yeast and fermentation is essential for any baker looking to create exceptional bread. By mastering the principles of yeast selection, fermentation control, and dough handling, you can achieve consistent and delicious results. Each step, from mixing and kneading to proofing and baking, plays a vital role in the final product. Embrace the science and art of yeast and fermentation, and you'll unlock the full potential of your bread-making skills. As you become more comfortable with the fundamentals of yeast and fermentation, experimenting with advanced techniques can further enhance your baking repertoire. One such technique is autolyse, a process involving a rest period after initially mixing flour and water but before adding yeast and salt. During this rest, the flour hydrates fully and gluten starts to develop, resulting in a dough that is easier to shape and handle. This method can improve the texture and flavor of the final loaf by promoting a more even fermentation and a well-developed gluten network.

Basic White Bread

Basic white bread, with its soft crumb and golden crust, remains a beloved staple in households around the world. Its simplicity belies the mastery required to perfect it, and understanding the fundamental processes involved can transform your baking from ordinary to exceptional. This chapter will guide you through the essential steps, techniques, and tips necessary to bake a loaf of basic white bread that is both delicious and visually appealing.

The foundation of any good loaf of white bread begins with the ingredients. The primary components are flour, water, yeast, salt, and sometimes a bit of sugar and fat. Each ingredient plays a crucial role in the bread-making process. Flour provides the structure, water hydrates the flour to develop gluten, yeast acts as the leavening agent, and salt adds flavor while controlling yeast activity. Sugar, often added in small amounts, feeds the yeast and enhances browning, while fat, such as butter or oil, adds richness and improves the bread's texture.

Selecting the right flour is essential. Bread flour, with its higher protein content, is ideal for white bread as it develops a stronger gluten network, resulting in a chewier texture and better rise. All-purpose flour can also be used, though the final loaf may be slightly less chewy. For a truly exceptional loaf, consider using unbleached flour, which retains more of the wheat's natural flavor and nutrients.

The first step in making basic white bread is to activate the yeast. If you're using active dry yeast, dissolve it in warm water (about 110°F or 43°C) with a teaspoon of sugar. Let it sit for about 5-10 minutes until it becomes frothy and bubbly, indicating that the yeast is alive and active. Instant yeast, on the other hand, can be mixed directly with the dry ingredients, saving a step and some time.

Once the yeast is ready, mix it with the flour, salt, and any additional ingredients such as sugar or fat. Begin to add water gradually, mixing until a rough dough forms. The amount of water needed can vary based on the type of flour and the humidity of your environment, so it's important to add it slowly and adjust as necessary. The dough should be slightly sticky but not overly wet.

Kneading is a critical step that develops the gluten, giving the bread its structure and chew. Turn the dough out onto a floured surface and knead it for about 10 minutes until it becomes smooth and elastic. You can test if the dough is ready by performing the windowpane test: stretch a small piece of dough between your fingers. If it forms a thin, translucent membrane without tearing, it's adequately kneaded.

After kneading, place the dough in a lightly oiled bowl, cover it with a damp cloth or plastic wrap, and let it rise in a warm, draft-free area. This first rise, known as bulk fermentation, typically takes about 1 to 2 hours, or until the dough has doubled in size. The yeast ferments the sugars in the flour, producing carbon dioxide that gets trapped in the gluten network, causing the dough to expand.

Once the dough has risen, gently punch it down to release the excess gas and turn it out onto a lightly floured surface. Shape the dough into a loaf by flattening it into a rectangle, folding the sides in, and rolling it tightly from one end to the other. Pinch the seams to seal them and place the loaf seam-side down in a greased loaf pan. Cover it again and let it rise for the second time, which usually takes about 30 to 60 minutes, or until it has risen just above the top of the pan.

While the dough is proofing, preheat your oven to 375°F (190°C). A well-preheated oven ensures an initial burst of heat, or oven spring, which helps the bread rise further and set its structure. Just before baking, you can score the top of the loaf with a sharp knife or razor blade. This scoring allows the bread to expand properly and gives it a professional appearance.

Baking typically takes about 30 to 35 minutes. The bread is done when it has a rich, golden-brown crust and sounds hollow when tapped on the bottom. An internal temperature of around 200°F (93°C) confirms that the bread is fully baked. Remove the loaf from the pan immediately after baking and let it cool on a wire rack. This cooling period is crucial as it allows the crumb to set and prevents it from becoming gummy.

Patience is key when it comes to slicing your freshly baked bread. Slicing too soon can result in a squashed loaf with a dense texture. Allow the bread to cool completely, which usually takes about an hour. This wait can be challenging, but it's essential for achieving the best texture and flavor.

Storing your homemade white bread properly will keep it fresh for several days. Once completely cool, store it in a bread box or a loosely wrapped plastic bag at room temperature. Avoid refrigerating the bread, as this can cause it to dry out and become stale more quickly. For longer storage, consider freezing the bread. Slice it before freezing, so you can easily thaw individual slices as needed.

Basic white bread is incredibly versatile and can be adapted to suit your tastes and needs. Adding ingredients such as herbs, cheese, garlic, or olives can create a variety of flavored loaves. You can also experiment with different shapes, such as rolls, braids, or baguettes. The techniques and principles remain the same, but the variations are endless.

A well-made loaf of white bread can serve as the foundation for countless meals. From simple toast with butter to gourmet sandwiches, its soft, tender crumb and mild flavor make it a favorite for many. Understanding the science and techniques behind bread-making not only improves your results but also deepens your appreciation for this age-old craft.

Baking bread is both an art and a science. Each step, from selecting ingredients to the final bake, requires attention to detail and a bit of intuition. With practice, you'll develop the skills and confidence to bake bread that rivals that of professional bakers. Remember that even experienced bakers encounter occasional challenges, but each loaf is an opportunity to learn and improve.

As you continue your bread-making journey, don't be afraid to experiment and make the process your own. Whether you're baking for family, friends, or simply for the joy of it, the satisfaction of pulling a beautiful, fragrant loaf from the oven is unparalleled. Embrace the process, savor the results, and share the love of homemade bread with those around you. To truly master the art of basic white bread, consider the subtle adjustments and personal touches that can elevate your loaf from good to extraordinary. Paying attention to every detail, from ingredient quality to handling the dough, will make a significant difference in your final product.

Whole Wheat Bread

Whole wheat bread, known for its robust flavor and nutritional benefits, is a favorite among health-conscious bakers. Crafting a perfect loaf requires understanding the unique properties of whole wheat flour and mastering techniques that balance its dense texture with a satisfying rise. This chapter will guide you through the intricacies of making whole wheat bread, offering practical tips and insights to ensure your success.

The foundation of whole wheat bread lies in the flour. Whole wheat flour includes the entire grain—bran, germ, and endosperm—providing more fiber, vitamins, and minerals compared to refined flours. However, these benefits come with challenges. The bran and germ in whole wheat flour can interfere with gluten development, resulting in a denser loaf. To counteract this, it's crucial to use fresh, high-quality whole wheat flour and consider blending it with bread flour to improve the dough's elasticity and rise.

Selecting the right flour is just the beginning. Hydration plays a significant role in whole wheat bread. Whole wheat flour absorbs more water than white flour due to its higher fiber content. A higher hydration dough can help achieve a softer crumb, but too much water can lead to a sticky, unmanageable dough. Start with a hydration level of around 70-75%, adjusting as needed based on the dough's feel and your baking environment.

Yeast is another critical component. Active dry yeast or instant yeast works well for whole wheat bread. Ensure your yeast is fresh and active by proofing it in warm water with a bit of honey or sugar. This step not only activates the yeast but also provides a slight sweetness that complements the hearty flavor of whole wheat.

Once your yeast is ready, combine it with the flour, water, salt, and a bit of fat such as olive oil or butter. The fat helps tenderize the crumb and adds richness to the flavor. Mixing the ingredients until they form a shaggy dough is the first step. Letting this mixture rest, a process known as autolyse, allows the flour to fully hydrate and the gluten to start developing. A 20-30 minute autolyse can make kneading easier and improve the dough's texture.

Kneading whole wheat dough requires attention and patience. The bran in whole wheat flour can cut through gluten strands, so kneading should be gentle yet effective. A typical kneading time of 10-15 minutes helps develop sufficient gluten. The dough will remain slightly tacky due to the high hydration, but it should become smooth and elastic. Using a stand mixer with a dough hook can simplify this process, but hand-kneading provides a tangible sense of progress and dough development.

Fermentation is where the magic happens. Place the kneaded dough in a lightly oiled bowl, cover it, and let it rise until doubled in size. This first rise, or bulk fermentation, typically takes 1-2 hours depending on the ambient temperature. A slower, cooler rise can enhance the bread's flavor, so consider refrigerating the dough overnight for an extended fermentation.

After the first rise, gently deflate the dough and shape it into a loaf. Shaping whole wheat dough can be challenging due to its density, but proper technique ensures an even crumb and good oven spring. Flatten the dough into a rectangle, fold it like an envelope, and roll it tightly. Pinch the seams to seal and place the loaf in a greased pan for the second rise. This proofing stage usually takes 45-60 minutes, or until the dough has risen just above the pan's rim.

Preheat your oven to 375°F (190°C) during the final proof. A hot oven is essential for good oven spring and crust development. Scoring the top of the loaf with a sharp knife or razor blade allows controlled expansion during baking.

Baking whole wheat bread usually takes 35-40 minutes. The loaf should have a deep, golden-brown crust and sound hollow when tapped on the bottom. For an accurate measure, the internal temperature should reach around 200°F (93°C). Immediately remove the bread from the pan and cool on a wire rack to prevent a soggy bottom.

Patience is key when it comes to slicing your whole wheat bread. Allow the loaf to cool completely, typically for at least an hour. This cooling period lets the crumb set and enhances the bread's texture and flavor.

Storing whole wheat bread properly will keep it fresh and flavorful. Once cooled, store the bread in a bread box or a loosely wrapped plastic bag at room temperature. Avoid refrigeration, as it can cause the bread to dry out. For longer storage, freeze the bread in slices or whole loaves. Thawing slices at room temperature or toasting them directly from frozen ensures convenience and freshness.

Whole wheat bread is highly versatile. Its nutty flavor and hearty texture make it suitable for a variety of culinary uses. Whether you're making sandwiches, toast, or breadcrumbs, whole wheat bread adds a nutritious and flavorful element to your meals.

Experimenting with whole wheat bread can lead to delightful discoveries. Adding seeds, nuts, or dried fruit can enhance the flavor and nutritional profile. Incorporating ingredients like honey, molasses, or yogurt can introduce new dimensions to the taste and texture. Adjusting the hydration, fermentation time, and baking techniques allows you to tailor the bread to your preferences.

Understanding the science behind whole wheat bread helps in troubleshooting potential issues. If your bread is too dense, consider increasing the hydration, kneading more thoroughly, or blending with bread flour. If it lacks flavor, a longer fermentation or the addition of natural sweeteners may help. Keeping a baking journal to record your process and results can be invaluable for continuous improvement.

Baking whole wheat bread is a rewarding endeavor. Each loaf you bake not only provides nourishment but also reflects your growing skills and understanding of the craft. The process, from mixing the dough to the final bake, is a journey of learning and satisfaction. Sharing your homemade bread with friends and family brings joy and a sense of accomplishment.

As you continue to bake whole wheat bread, you'll develop a deeper appreciation for the nuances of the process. Embrace each step, from selecting ingredients to mastering techniques, with curiosity and dedication. The skills you acquire will serve as a foundation for exploring other types of bread and expanding your baking repertoire.

Bread-making is both an art and a science. Whole wheat bread, with its rich flavor and nutritional benefits, embodies this balance beautifully. By understanding the properties of whole wheat flour and perfecting your techniques, you can create loaves that are both delicious and wholesome. Enjoy the journey, savor the results, and continue to share the love of homemade bread with those around you. Happy baking! Whole wheat bread offers endless possibilities for customization and improvement. As you gain confidence in your baking skills, don't hesitate to experiment with different variations and techniques to make each loaf uniquely your own.

Artisan Sourdough Techniques

Artisan sourdough bread embodies the essence of traditional baking, combining simple ingredients with time-honored techniques to create loaves with complex flavors and satisfying textures. Mastering sourdough requires patience, attention to detail, and a willingness to learn from each bake. This chapter delves into the essential techniques for making artisan sourdough, from nurturing a starter to achieving the perfect crust and crumb.

The heart of sourdough baking is the starter—a living mixture of flour and water that captures wild yeast and bacteria from the environment. This culture ferments over time, developing the characteristic tangy flavor and leavening power that defines sourdough bread. To create a starter, mix equal parts whole grain flour and water in a jar, cover loosely, and let it sit at room temperature. Feed the starter daily with fresh flour and water, discarding half of the mixture each time. Within a week, you should have a bubbly, active starter ready for baking.

Once you have an active starter, it's time to prepare the dough. Begin by mixing the starter with flour and water to form a shaggy mass. This initial mixing stage, known as autolyse, allows the flour to fully hydrate and the gluten to begin developing. Let the mixture rest for 30 minutes to an hour. After the autolyse, add salt and a bit more water to the dough. Salt not only enhances flavor but also strengthens the gluten structure, contributing to a better rise and texture.

Kneading sourdough dough differs from traditional methods due to its high hydration level. Instead of vigorous kneading, use a series of stretches and folds to develop the gluten network. Every 30 minutes for about two hours, stretch the dough from one side and fold it over itself, rotating the bowl each time. This gentle technique builds strength and elasticity without overworking the dough.

Fermentation is a crucial phase in sourdough baking. After the initial stretch and fold sessions, let the dough ferment at room temperature until it has doubled in size. This bulk fermentation can take anywhere from 4 to 6 hours, depending on the ambient temperature and the vitality of your starter. For a more pronounced flavor, consider a cold fermentation by refrigerating the dough overnight. This slow fermentation process allows the flavors to deepen and develop complexity.

Shaping the dough is an art in itself. After the bulk fermentation, gently turn the dough onto a lightly floured surface. Pre-shape it by folding the edges towards the center, creating a taut surface. Let it rest for 20-30 minutes. Then, final shape the dough by repeating the folding process, ensuring a tight, smooth surface. Place the shaped dough into a proofing basket or a bowl lined with a floured cloth, seam side up. This final proofing stage helps the dough relax and rise further, setting the structure for the final bake.

Scoring the dough before baking allows for controlled expansion and enhances the bread's aesthetic appeal. Use a sharp knife or a razor blade to make shallow cuts on the surface of the dough. Traditional patterns like a simple slash, a cross, or a leaf motif not only look beautiful but also guide the dough's expansion in the oven.

Baking sourdough bread requires a hot, steamy environment to achieve a crisp crust and good oven spring. Preheat your oven to 475°F (245°C) with a baking stone or a heavy baking sheet inside. Place a shallow pan of water in the oven to create steam. Transfer the dough onto the preheated stone or sheet, either by flipping it from the proofing basket or using parchment paper for support. Bake at high heat for the first 15-20 minutes to maximize oven spring, then reduce the temperature to 450°F (230°C) and continue baking for another 20-25 minutes until the crust is deep golden brown and the loaf sounds hollow when tapped.

Patience is essential after baking. Allow the loaf to cool completely on a wire rack before slicing. This cooling period lets the crumb set and the flavors to mature. Cutting into the bread too soon can result in a gummy texture and a less satisfying eating experience.

Sourdough bread-making is a journey of discovery. Each bake offers new insights and opportunities for refinement. Keeping a detailed baking journal can be invaluable. Note the specifics of each bake—flour types, hydration levels, fermentation times, and ambient conditions. This record helps identify patterns, understand the dough's behavior, and make informed adjustments for future bakes.

One of the joys of artisan sourdough is its versatility. Experiment with different flours, such as rye, spelt, or whole wheat, to add unique flavors and textures.

Incorporate seeds, nuts, or dried fruits for added interest and nutrition. Adjust the hydration to create a dough that suits your preferences, whether for a rustic, open crumb or a tighter, sandwich-friendly loaf.

Sharing your sourdough creations with family and friends is one of the most rewarding aspects of baking. A beautifully crafted loaf of sourdough is a gift that embodies time, effort, and love. Whether you bring it to a dinner party, give it as a heartfelt present, or simply enjoy it at home, the act of sharing enhances the joy of baking and connects you with others.

Sourdough's rich history and cultural significance add depth to the experience of baking. From ancient civilizations to modern kitchens, sourdough has been a staple in diets worldwide. Understanding the historical context and traditional methods can deepen your appreciation and inspire your baking journey.

Maintaining a healthy starter is crucial for consistent results. Feed your starter regularly, adjusting the feeding schedule based on its activity and your baking frequency. If you bake often, keep the starter at room temperature and feed it daily. For less frequent baking, store the starter in the refrigerator and feed it weekly, allowing it to come to room temperature and become active before use.

Troubleshooting common sourdough issues is part of the learning process. If your bread is too dense, it may need more fermentation time or stronger gluten development. A flat loaf could indicate over-proofing or insufficient shaping. Excessive sourness might result from too long fermentation or an overly acidic starter. Adjusting variables like temperature, timing, and ingredient ratios can help you achieve the desired balance.

The tactile experience of working with dough, the anticipation during fermentation, and the satisfaction of pulling a perfectly baked loaf from the oven are unmatched. Each step, from feeding the starter to the final bake, is an opportunity to engage with a centuries-old tradition and create something uniquely your own.

Artisan sourdough techniques combine science and artistry, transforming simple ingredients into a complex, flavorful loaf. Through practice and experimentation, you'll develop a deep understanding of the dough, honing your skills and refining your approach. Celebrate each success, learn from each challenge, and enjoy the timeless craft of sourdough baking. Happy baking! Embracing the artisan sourdough journey opens a world of creativity and satisfaction. As you become more comfortable with the foundational techniques, you can explore advanced methods and variations to elevate your bread-making skills even further.

Enriched Breads: Brioche and Challah

Baking enriched breads like brioche and challah introduces a delightful blend of tradition, technique, and indulgence. These breads, characterized by their rich ingredients such as eggs, butter, and sugar, offer a tender crumb and a nuanced flavor profile. Perfecting these loaves requires an understanding of their distinct dough properties and baking processes. This chapter guides you through the intricacies of making brioche and challah, from mixing and kneading to shaping and baking.

Brioche is a luxurious French bread that combines the richness of butter and eggs with a light, airy texture. To begin, gather high-quality ingredients: all-purpose flour, eggs, butter, sugar, milk, salt, and yeast. The quality of these ingredients significantly impacts the final product, so opt for fresh, high-fat butter and farm-fresh eggs if possible.

Start by activating the yeast. Warm the milk to about 110°F (43°C), ensuring it's not too hot to kill the yeast or too cold to activate it. Dissolve a teaspoon of sugar in the milk, then sprinkle the yeast on top, allowing it to bloom for about 5-10 minutes until frothy. This step ensures that your yeast is alive and ready to leaven the dough.

In a large mixing bowl, combine the flour, sugar, and salt. Create a well in the center and add the yeast mixture and lightly beaten eggs. Using a dough hook attachment on a stand mixer, mix on low speed until the ingredients come together into a shaggy dough. Gradually add softened butter, a few tablespoons at a time, allowing each addition to fully incorporate before adding more. This gradual incorporation is crucial for achieving the smooth, elastic texture characteristic of brioche.

Once all the butter is added, increase the mixing speed to medium and knead the dough for about 10-15 minutes. The dough should become smooth, shiny, and elastic, and it should pass the "windowpane test"—when stretched, it should form a thin, translucent membrane without tearing. This indicates proper gluten development, essential for the bread's structure.

Transfer the dough to a lightly greased bowl, cover it with plastic wrap, and let it rise in a warm, draft-free area until it has doubled in size, about 1-2 hours. For a more pronounced flavor, you can refrigerate the dough overnight for a slow, cold fermentation. This extended fermentation period allows the flavors to develop more deeply.

After the first rise, gently deflate the dough and turn it onto a floured surface. Divide it into the desired portions, depending on whether you're making a loaf, buns, or individual brioche à tête. Shape the dough into tight, smooth balls, ensuring a taut surface to encourage a good rise in the oven. Place the shaped dough into greased molds or on a baking sheet lined with parchment paper.

Let the shaped dough proof for a second time, approximately 1-2 hours, until it has visibly puffed up. Preheat your oven to 375°F (190°C) during the final proofing stage. Just before baking, brush the tops of the brioche with an egg wash (a beaten egg mixed with a tablespoon of water), which gives the bread a beautiful, glossy finish.

Bake the brioche in the preheated oven for 20-25 minutes, or until the tops are a deep golden brown and the internal temperature reaches 190°F (88°C). Allow the brioche to cool in the molds for a few minutes before transferring to a wire rack to cool completely. The result is a rich, buttery bread with a delicate crumb and a beautiful golden crust.

Challah, a traditional Jewish braided bread, is equally rich but with a slightly different flavor profile and structure. It is typically made with oil instead of butter, giving it a lighter, fluffier texture. Begin by gathering ingredients: all-purpose flour, eggs, sugar, oil, water, salt, and yeast.

Activate the yeast in warm water with a teaspoon of sugar, just as you would for brioche. In a large mixing bowl, combine the flour, sugar, and salt. Create a well in the center and add the yeast mixture, oil, and lightly beaten eggs. Mix the ingredients together until a rough dough forms, then knead on a floured surface or using a stand mixer with a dough hook attachment for about 10 minutes. The dough should be smooth, elastic, and slightly tacky.

Place the dough in a lightly greased bowl, cover it with plastic wrap, and let it rise in a warm place until it has doubled in size, about 1-2 hours. After the first rise, gently deflate the dough and turn it onto a floured surface. Divide the dough into equal portions, depending on the number of strands you want for your braid. Traditional challah is made with three, four, or six strands, each offering a different visual and structural complexity.

Roll each portion into a long rope, making sure they are of equal length and thickness. To braid a three-strand challah, pinch the tops of the ropes together and braid them as you would hair, tucking the ends underneath to secure. For a four-strand braid, arrange the ropes in a crisscross pattern and follow a specific over-under braiding technique to create a symmetrical loaf. A six-strand braid requires a more intricate pattern, but the result is a beautifully complex loaf.

Place the braided challah on a baking sheet lined with parchment paper, cover it loosely with plastic wrap, and let it rise for a second time until it has doubled in size, about 1-2 hours. Preheat your oven to 350°F (175°C) during the final proofing stage. Brush the loaf with an egg wash, and for a traditional touch, sprinkle with sesame or poppy seeds.

Bake the challah in the preheated oven for 25-30 minutes, or until the top is a deep golden brown and the internal temperature reaches 190°F (88°C). Allow the loaf to cool on a wire rack before slicing. The result is a soft, slightly sweet bread with a tender crumb and a beautiful, shiny crust.

Both brioche and challah offer opportunities for variation and creativity. For brioche, consider adding sweet or savory fillings such as chocolate, fruit preserves, or cheese. Challah can be enriched with raisins, honey, or spices like cinnamon for a festive touch. These variations not only enhance the flavor but also add a personal touch to your baking.

Understanding the principles behind enriched doughs is key to mastering these breads. The high fat content from butter or oil, combined with eggs and sugar, enriches the dough, resulting in a tender, flavorful crumb. The dough's hydration level and gluten development are crucial for achieving the desired texture and structure. Proper kneading, rising, and proofing times are essential to ensure the dough is well-developed and ready for baking.

Enriched breads like brioche and challah are more than just delicious treats; they are a testament to the art and science of baking. Each step, from mixing the dough to shaping and baking, requires attention to detail and a deep understanding of the ingredients and processes involved. As you practice and refine your techniques, you'll gain confidence and mastery over these rich, flavorful breads.

In conclusion, baking enriched breads such as brioche and challah is a rewarding and enriching experience. These breads, with their rich ingredients and intricate techniques, offer a delightful challenge for any baker. By understanding the unique properties of enriched doughs and perfecting your methods, you can create stunning loaves that are as beautiful as they are delicious. Embrace the process, experiment with variations, and enjoy the satisfaction of baking these traditional, indulgent breads. Enriched breads like brioche and challah also carry cultural and historical significance. Brioche, with its roots in France, was once considered a luxury bread reserved for the wealthy. It has evolved over centuries, influencing various regional recipes and techniques. The bread's rich, buttery profile makes it a versatile base for both sweet and savory dishes. Brioche buns are often used for gourmet burgers, while slices of brioche make an indulgent French toast or bread pudding.

Troubleshooting Yeast Bread Issues

Baking yeast bread is an art that combines precise measurements, careful attention to detail, and a touch of intuition. Despite best efforts, sometimes issues arise that can turn what was supposed to be a beautiful loaf into a disappointing result. Troubleshooting these problems is crucial for improving your baking skills and achieving consistently excellent bread. Understanding common issues and their solutions can transform your baking experience and elevate your bread-making prowess.

One of the most frequent issues novice bakers encounter is poor yeast activation. Yeast is a living organism that needs the right conditions to thrive. Using water that is too hot can kill the yeast, while water that is too cold can fail to activate it. Ideally, the water should be between 105°F and 110°F (40°C to 43°C). Always use a thermometer to ensure the correct temperature. If, after 10 minutes, your yeast mixture isn't foamy, the yeast might be dead or the water temperature incorrect. Start fresh with new yeast and double-check the temperature.

Another common problem is dough that fails to rise adequately. This can be due to several factors, including expired yeast, insufficient kneading, or an unsuitable environment for fermentation. Always check the expiration date on your yeast before use. Ensure you knead the dough thoroughly to develop gluten, which traps gas bubbles produced by the yeast. The dough should be smooth and elastic. The rising environment should be warm and draft-free. If your kitchen is cold, consider placing the dough in an oven with just the oven light on or near a warm appliance.

Overproofing and underproofing dough are also frequent issues. Overproofed dough has risen too much and may collapse, resulting in dense bread with large, irregular holes. Underproofed dough hasn't risen enough, leading to dense bread with a tight crumb. To test if your dough has proofed enough, gently press your finger into it. If the indentation springs back slowly and partially, it's ready. If it springs back quickly, it needs more time. If it doesn't spring back at all, it's overproofed. Adjust proofing times according to your kitchen environment and always keep an eye on the dough.

Dense or heavy bread can be a sign of insufficient kneading, improper flour-to-water ratio, or issues with yeast. Ensure you knead the dough until it passes the windowpane test—stretch a small piece of dough until it's thin and translucent without tearing. This indicates proper gluten development. Measure flour and water accurately; too much flour can make the dough stiff and hard to rise. If your bread is consistently dense, consider using bread flour, which has a higher protein content, aiding gluten development.

Cracked or split crusts are often caused by improper scoring or the dough drying out during proofing. Scoring allows the bread to expand properly in the oven. Use a sharp blade to make decisive, quick slashes. Cover the dough with a damp cloth or plastic wrap during proofing to prevent it from drying out. If the crust splits despite scoring, it might be due to the oven being too hot at the start. Try lowering the initial temperature slightly and use steam during the first part of baking to keep the crust flexible.

Another issue is bread with a gummy interior, which can result from underbaking or cutting the bread too soon after baking. Ensure your oven is properly calibrated and always preheat it fully. Bread is done when it sounds hollow when tapped on the bottom and has an internal temperature of about 200°F (93°C). Allow the bread to cool completely on a wire rack before cutting. Cutting into hot bread traps steam inside, creating a gummy texture.

If your bread has an off flavor, it might be due to the yeast or improper storage. Fresh yeast should have a pleasant, slightly yeasty smell. If it smells off, it's likely expired. Store yeast in the refrigerator or freezer to extend its shelf life. Improperly stored flour can also develop rancid flavors. Keep flour in an airtight container in a cool, dark place. For long-term storage, consider refrigerating or freezing flour.

Uneven crumb structure can be caused by inconsistent kneading or proofing. Ensure you knead the dough evenly and give it enough time to develop gluten. Avoid adding too much flour during kneading; the dough should be slightly sticky but manageable. During shaping, handle the dough gently to avoid deflating it. Allow the dough to rise fully to ensure even air distribution.

If your bread is too dry, it could be due to overbaking or using too much flour. Always measure ingredients accurately and avoid adding extra flour unless absolutely necessary. Cover the dough with a damp cloth during proofing to retain moisture. Consider adding a bit of fat, such as butter or oil, to the dough to help retain moisture. Monitor baking times closely and remove the bread from the oven as soon as it's done.

Blistered crust can result from overproofing or a too-cold oven. If the dough is overproofed, it can develop small bubbles on the surface that turn into blisters in the oven. Ensure your oven is fully preheated to the correct temperature before baking. If using a baking stone, allow ample time for it to heat thoroughly.

Sourdough bread can present unique challenges, such as weak or inactive starter, overly sour flavor, or poor oven spring. Maintain a healthy starter by feeding it regularly and using it when it's at its peak activity. An overly sour flavor can result from extended fermentation times or too much starter. Adjust fermentation times to suit your taste and use less starter if needed. Poor oven spring can be due to underproofing or insufficient steam. Ensure the dough is proofed correctly and use steam during the first part of baking.

Incorporating these troubleshooting techniques into your baking routine will help you diagnose and correct common issues, leading to better results. Pay close attention to the details of each step, from yeast activation to final baking. Keep a baking journal to track your process, noting any adjustments and their outcomes. This practice can help you identify patterns and refine your techniques over time.

Baking yeast bread is a journey of continuous learning and improvement. Embrace the challenges and use each loaf as an opportunity to grow and enhance your skills. With patience, practice, and attention to detail, you'll be able to troubleshoot and resolve issues, creating beautiful, delicious bread every time. Understanding how to troubleshoot yeast bread issues is invaluable for any baker aiming to achieve consistently high-quality results. By honing your skills and applying practical solutions, you can turn potential setbacks into valuable learning experiences.